“Honesty, candor and practicality . . . ”

“I’ve known the Strauss family for many years. When he speaks, there is authority because the family lives out their Christian faith on a day to day basis. This is not theory. This is practiced too.”

Luis Palau
International Evangelist

“The Strausses prove, with graphic detail, what I have long believed: Everybody’s incompatible. But they also prove, in intimate detail, that when two people – a sinful man and a sinful woman – are saved by grace and make up their minds to do the will of God, their marriage is an increasingly beautiful thing. I’m glad they were willing to tell their story.”

Elisabeth Elliot
Author, Speaker

“Picture the dignified Richard Strauss cutting up a leftover baked potato for his breakfast. Not any potato mind you, but one Mary intended to use in a different meal later that day! The dilemmas and delights of marriage and family abound in this attractive and intimate book. Richard and Mary share their lives in honesty, candor and practicality, inserting poignant glimpses of the gospel at appropriate points.

“The short chapters can be read at one sitting and, if possible, husband and wives should read them together. The book is easy to read, upbeat and bright and the ‘action points’ provide opportunities for immediate implementation. An outstanding treatment of 1 Corinthians 13 comes complete with a ‘love test.’

“Particularly helpful to students and young couples, the book also speaks to families who have already entered middle age. Many husbands and wives will identif
and Mary paint for us in *When Tu*

Dr. Kenneth
Chairman, I
Dallas Theo

Here's Life books by Richard Strauss

Getting Along With Each Other

When Two Walk Together

When Two Walk Together

Richard and Mary
STRAUSS

First printing, August 1988

Published by
HERE'S LIFE PUBLISHERS, INC.
P. O. Box 1576
San Bernardino, CA 92402

Printed in the United States of America

Library of Congress Cataloging-in-Publication Data
Strauss, Richard L.
When two walk together.
1. Marriage—Religious aspects—Christianity.
2. Love—Religious aspects—Christianity. I. Strauss, Mary (Mary G.) II. Title
BV835.S878 1988 88-760
ISBN 0-89840-216-6 (pbk.)

For More Information, Write:
L.I.F.E.—P.O. Box A399, Sydney South 2000, Australia
Campus Crusade for Christ of Canada—Box 300, Vancouver, B.C., V6C 2X3, Canada
Campus Crusade for Christ—Pearl Assurance House, 4 Temple Row, Birmingham, B2 5HG, England
Lay Institute for Evangelism—P.O. Box 8786, Auckland 3, New Zealand
Campus Crusade for Christ—P.O. Box 240, Colombo Court Post Office, Singapore 9117
Great Commission Movement of Nigeria—P.O. Box 500, Jos, Plateau State Nigeria, West Africa
Campus Crusade for Christ International—Arrowhead Springs, San Bernardino, CA 92414, U.S.A.

Contents

Our marriage wasn't supposed to be like this. How could it have turned out this bad?

1

ONE THIN DIME

Richard, look at this. There's a two-for-one ad from El Chico Restaurant in the newspaper tonight. I think maybe we can afford that. And Steve had a pretty good nap today. He should be good in the restaurant. Do you think we should go?"

My reply was instantaneous: "Let's do it!" Mexican food was getting to be my favorite.

So we went. It was a delicious dinner. And such a bargain! Two meals for the price of one. And in addition to that, we fed our two-year-old son off our plates. It was actually three meals for the price of one. As poor seminary students, we were always looking for a bargain, and we had surely found one.

Our stomachs were filled, and we were all quite contented as we started out of the restaurant. I stopped at the cash register to pay the bill, while Mary took Steve on to the car. It had been a pleasant evening out for all of us, a rarity with our busy schedule. And I was feeling proud that we were able to pull it off on such a limited budget.

I slid behind the steering wheel of the car and handed the change to Mary. She was good with figures, and I appreciated her willingness to handle the family finances. It wasn't easy for me to carry a full academic load at Dallas Seminary, work twenty-five hours a week to support my family, and still try to spend some quality time with them. She took some of the pressure off of me by keeping the books and paying the bills, and she did it well.

As I started the car, I saw out of the corner of my eye that she was counting the change I had given her. "Didn't you count this in the restaurant?" she asked. "You're a dime short." She sounded angry and upset. "No," I replied. "I assumed the cashier gave me the right amount." "Well, she didn't. She gypped you a dime. And I think you ought to go back in there and get it."

"Mary, I'm not going back in there and ask for a dime. We fed three people for the price of one. How can you say that they cheated us?" The very thought of going back into the restaurant and asking for that dime struck terror into me. I didn't have the confidence nor the assertiveness to handle a situation like that. But I wasn't going to admit that. I would simply keep pointing out to her how ridiculous it would be to go back and ask for the dime when the restaurant had already given us such a good deal. It wasn't worth the effort.

Before I realized what was happening, our 1951 Plymouth had turned into a battleground. Mary was literally shouting at me. "Maybe a dime is not important to you, but you're not the one who has to stretch the money. Every *penny* counts. And that's ten pennies! You don't understand how difficult it is to make ends meet with your paycheck. And if you don't care any more about it than that, then you can just handle the money yourself. I'm sick and tired of the hassle."

I could feel myself getting more and more angry as I defended my refusal to go back for the dime, and my voice was getting louder and louder as I tried to make her see how unreasonable she was acting. The angrier I got, the more hostile she became, and the argument was getting hotter by the second. Our young son was standing on the front seat of the car between us (before the days of seat belts) taking it all in. His head was swinging back and forth from one of us to the other, and his eyes were as wide as saucers.

Arguments like this had become the normal pattern of our marriage. They would leave us feeling bitter and alienated from each other, and the coolness would last for days at a time. Neither of us liked it that way, but we didn't know how to change it. It wasn't supposed to be like this. We were the ideal couple—I was the preacher's kid—a good kid. My father used to say that I never gave him a day of trouble in my whole life. Mary was considered to be one of the more spiritually minded young people in our church. We had come from almost identical backgrounds, and we were supposed to have the perfect marriage. How could it have turned out to be this bad? Maybe our two worlds were not as much alike as we thought they were . . .

I was a pastor—wasn't my marriage supposed to be one of perfect harmony?

2

RICHARD'S WORLD

It was in Philadelphia, Pennsylvania that I uttered my first squeals—actually in the Women's General Hospital (and was I ever embarrassed!). My dad was an enthusiastic, outgoing salesman at Sears, and my mother a quiet, more introverted housewife, both of whom dearly loved the Lord. Dad was attending evening classes at Philadelphia School of the Bible and looked forward to entering the ministry.

I have happy memories of walking to the corner to meet him after work, and climbing on the running-board of his car (remember them?) for the short ride home. He held me securely with one arm as he drove with the other. I also remember happy times with my widowed maternal grandfather and a bachelor uncle who lived with us during my early childhood years.

Along with the happy times, however, I remember being rather shy and self-conscious, with a poor self-image. I lived in the shadow of a father with a strong personality, who was usually at the center of everything that was happening, and who would gain increasing national prominence as an outstanding preacher and Bible teacher. I grew up thinking that I would never measure up to Dad's standard. I can remember wanting to please him, but seldom being sure that I had.

The one experience from my childhood that overshadows

all others in my thinking occurred the day I arrived home from school and found the door to our row-house locked. That was different. I rang the doorbell and pounded on the door (it was a French door with glass panels from top to bottom), but nobody answered. As a little second grader, I could feel fear overtake me. Where were my parents? I pounded harder and accidently broke one of the glass door panels. That's when I panicked and took off running toward a friend's house three blocks away. Somewhere enroute it dawned on me that I had been told to go there if ever my parents were not at home after school. The rest of the afternoon was spent playing with my friend.

When my parents returned home that evening, they asked me if I knew how the window had been broken, and I told them that I saw a kid throw a snowball through the glass. They were reasonably sure I was lying since there was no puddle of water on the inside, but they couldn't prove it. So the incident was dropped . . . until the following summer. That's when a neighbor lady who happened to be chatting with my mother told her that she saw me break the glass. My lie was exposed, and lying was totally unacceptable behavior in my family.

You can be sure that I was not looking forward to Dad coming home from work that day. And he did exactly what I expected him to do—he led me upstairs to his bedroom. I had been there before and knew what was coming. And it did. After explaining to me calmly why lying was unacceptable, he "drove the lesson home" with a spanking. Spankings were no fun, but somehow I sensed that Dad loved me even when he spanked me because tears streamed down his face. I never understood why it hurt him so much until God gave me children of my own.

But something else happened that day which turned out to be the most important and most pleasant experience of my entire life. When we each stopped crying, Dad used my lie to show me kindly and lovingly that I was a sinner and that I needed a Savior. He went on to explain that Jesus Christ had paid for my sin on the cross of Calvary and wanted to save me from its eternal penalty. If I would put my trust in Him, He would forgive me of all my sin, accept me as His very own child, and give me the gift of eternal life. We knelt down together beside the bed and Dad led me in a prayer of faith. While my understanding of eternal salvation would grow with the passing years, there is no doubt in my mind that Jesus Christ entered my life that day. And what He did on that occasion would ultimately become a major contributing factor in helping Mary and me solve our marital problems.

A clear understanding and a firm assurance of eternal salvation are essential ingredients for a successful marriage. It is difficult to reach out to our mates with forgiveness if we ourselves feel guilty before God. It is difficult to extend to them an attitude of acceptance when we ourselves feel rejected by God. It is difficult to be tolerant of their shortcomings when we feel as though God is angry and impatient with ours. It is difficult to offer them unconditional love if we feel that we have to perform to a certain level in order to earn God's love and favor.

But the assurance of our salvation can eliminate those problems. In Christ we are eternally forgiven and unconditionally loved and accepted. And when we have that confidence, we are free to relate unselfishly with our mates. Enjoying the reality of God's gracious salvation lays the foundation for healthy marital relationships.

It was some time before I understood fully what I possessed in Jesus Christ: that I am unconditionally accepted, with nothing to prove and nothing to lose, that it is Christ who lives in me and is willing to live through me, that all my personal needs for significance and worth are fully satisfied in my relationship with Him. Through my early years and on into my marriage I worried a great deal about what people thought of me and how they treated me. And this insecurity was the source of many marital conflicts. A more complete understanding would come in time, but it would never have been possible had I not first acknowledged my sin and put my trust in Christ as my personal Savior. The day Jesus Christ washed my sins away was crucial to eventually making our marriage work.

Like so many other children who have grown up in Christian homes, I cannot remember having a particularly warm and vital walk with God through my early teen years. But I did want to do the will of God. It was at a missionary conference when I was about fifteen years of age that I yielded myself to God and told Him I wanted to live my life for His glory. I didn't always do that, but God kept bringing me back to the commitment I had made. And while I considered other vocations, there was always a feeling deep within me that God would eventually lead me to serve Him in some kind of professional Christian ministry.

That's why the conflicts Mary and I were having seemed so devastating—since I was a seminary student, and later a pastor, wasn't my marriage supposed to be one of perfect harmony? Weren't we to be the model couple to our friends and congregation? Then why did we fight so much?

WALKING TOGETHER

If you have never trusted Jesus Christ as your personal Savior from sin, do it now. Acknowledge that your sin alienates you from God, that God's eternal, sinless Son paid the penalty you deserved when He died on Calvary's cross. Then put your faith in Him alone as your sin-bearer and deliverer from the guilt and condemnation of your sin. At that moment God will give you the gift of eternal life, and His Spirit will enter your life to enable you to do His will.

Mary's commitment to do the will of God would become one of the major factors in salvaging our marriage.

3

MARY'S WORLD

It was the Shirley Temple era and little girls with curly hair were "in." Mary's mother got her wish and gave birth to a blonde, curly haired baby whom friends would often compare to the famous little movie star. The birth took place in an apartment above a barber shop in the city of brotherly love.

From her earliest years she felt loved and accepted by her mother and her father. Being their first child, and the only child for eleven years as well as the first grandchild on either side, she was considered very special. "Isn't she cute!" people would exclaim. When she talked, everyone listened. They were building into her a strong self-image.

"It wasn't until I entered kindergarten that I discovered that the world didn't revolve around me," she says. "My kindergarten teacher had the audacity to tell me that I talked too much, and she even made me stand in the corner for disrupting the class. (Richard says she must have been a very courageous teacher to take me on like that!) But relating with friends was more important to me than pasting and finger-painting.

"Two important events occurred in my life at the tender age of six. The first, and most important, was putting my trust in Jesus Christ as Savior from sin. The presence of God's

Spirit within me would be the major factor in my life from that day on. The second was moving into the home of my paternal grandmother. My parents wanted to save enough money to build their own little dream home, and this seemed like the logical way to do it: Grandma could take care of me while Mother worked. Although I have not understood it until recent years, that was to have a lasting impact on my life.

"Grandmom was a Christian, but nobody had ever taught her how to apply the principles of Scripture to everyday living. She and my grandfather did not get along at all. They did not communicate with each other, and they slept in different bedrooms. Grandmom actually refused to let me talk to him.

"Her hostility and criticism were not only expressed toward my grandfather, however. There were times when she would get up and leave the room when my maternal grandmother came for a visit. And her extremely critical remarks and actions toward my friends are still vivid in my memory. There were a few of them whom she did not care for at all, and I can remember her making faces and sticking her tongue out at them. I tell you these things, not to belittle her, but to help you understand the emotional baggage that I brought with me into my marriage. It was during those years that I learned criticism as a way of life.

"As a child, summers were my favorite time, because summers meant *camp!* The one I liked best was Camp Sankanac, sponsored by the Bible Club Movement. One week at Sankanac stands above all others in my memory. A missionary from Africa was speaking on the will of God, and her message affected me powerfully. I had heard messages before on presenting my *body* to Christ, going wherever He wanted me to go and doing whatever He wanted me to do. But this time it was different. I saw clearly that God desired me to give my *will* to Him as well, to do what He wanted me to do whether it was what I wanted or not. I made that commitment. Psychologists would probably have labeled me a strong-willed child, but I honestly gave that will to God in the best way I knew how.

"One of my favorite pastimes as a young girl was reading, and missionary biographies were high on my list. The story of John and Betty Stam and their strong dedication to God's will helped to mold my life goals. The verse they had adopted before their martyrdom in China in 1934 became my life verse: '. . . so now also Christ shall be magnified in my body, whether it be by life or by death' (Philippians 1:20*b*). It seemed to me that one of life's highest callings for me would be to become a missionary or a pastor's wife. Those feelings may have been God's way of preparing me for the relationship He had planned for me in years to come."

Mary's commitment to do the will of God would become one of the major factors in salvaging our marriage. We have found that couples who are considering divorce often lack that commitment. Since it seems easier for them to call it quits than to work through the tough problems in their relationship, they take the path of least resistance and head for the lawyer's office, with little consideration for what God might want them to do. Had they ever settled this issue of yielding their wills to Him and letting Him rule their lives, it might have been different.

But the other side of Mary's personality—her critical nature—was to encounter the shyness and poor self-image I brought with me into our marriage. The result was like storm clouds that thunder in the sky when warm and cold fronts meet.

WALKING TOGETHER

If you have never genuinely yielded your will to Christ, won't you do it now? Then, whenever you face a decision or problem, pray, "Lord, I want to do Your will. Please show me Your heart's desire."

We seldom settled anything after we argued . . . it was a poor habit pattern that would carry over into our marriage.

4

THE TWO WORLDS MEET

It was shortly after I came to know Christ as my Savior that my father accepted the call to pastor the Calvary Baptist Church in Bristol, Pennsylvania. And other than being a preacher's kid, I lived a relatively normal childhood. I was in my early teens when Mary's father began building his dream house several miles south of Bristol. Her parents were both believers and one of their first priorities was to find a new church home. Here is how she remembers it:

"While looking through the church pages in the telephone directory, my mom found the listing of a church pastored by Lehman Strauss. In amazement she exclaimed, 'I used to know a Lehman Strauss when I was younger. His family lived around the corner from us, and my brothers and his brothers were friends. But from what I remember, he surely wouldn't be a minister. And yet it seems unlikely that there would be two men with that name. Let's go and see.'

"To our surprise it was the same Lehman Strauss mother had known when she was a young girl, now saved and serving the Lord. And so we all (mother, dad, two sisters and myself) settled into our new church home. It was difficult, as it was with most young high school girls, for me to break into the girls' clique at the church. The boys were much more accepting of me."

I can heartily agree with that. I still remember the first day Mary walked into church. My first thoughts were, "Now that's a cute little number; I'd like to get to know her better." Her vivacious, outgoing personality attracted me. And every time I looked at her, there were several guys around her. She seemed to be everything I was not, and opposites really do attract. But with my lack of confidence, I never made a move. She dated seven different boys in the first year she was there. And I just stood by and watched. Mary admits:

"I enjoyed the attention of all those guys. I was at the age when boys were becoming important. Richard was not entirely out of my mind during that year, however. There was something about him that I liked. He was the preacher's son, and he played an accordion in front of the whole church (that was a long time ago, before guitars were so popular; accordions were 'in' then). I enjoyed being in the limelight, and dating him would have given me some prominence."

So the scene was set for that fateful October hayride. Mary went with one of the other boys from the church, but I just went with the guys. Sometime during the evening she had a typical teenage spat with her date and they split up. That was just the opportunity I had been waiting for. I sat down beside her and we began to talk.

We don't remember how we got started, but we do remember that the conversation turned to spiritual things. One of the things we discussed was the difficulty of maintaining a strong testimony for Christ among our school friends. She impressed me with her love for the Lord and her desire to do His will. She was mischievous and talkative, and got into trouble with her teachers, and yet there was a spiritual depth in her that I wanted in the girl I eventually would marry. Our long and sometimes turbulent courtship began that night.

Our dating life was characteristic of most high school relationships. We attended rival high schools, so we did not see each other much during the week. But we spent a great deal of time together on weekends. And we talked for hours on the telephone. We both graciously offered to baby-sit our younger siblings for our parents on prayer meeting night so we could talk on the phone uninterrupted for the entire evening.

Three times during those high school years we broke off our relationship and Mary dated others. I had a couple of brief summer romances, but they meant very little to me. In the back of my mind I always though about getting back with Mary. I wanted her to be my girlfriend, and that was all that mattered to me. When we were going together, I usually wanted to go steady. It was selfish of me. As I look back on it now, I realize that it was my insecurity that made me hold on so tightly. And it led to repeated arguments.

Maybe Mary should explain it from her perspective. "I thought Richard was being possessive. I wanted to date other guys and also spend time with my girlfriends (by this time I had gotten into the clique). He didn't understand my wishes. It was frustrating to me, and I would vent my anger frequently."

Even when we were going steady, we didn't know how to communicate our feelings to each other without hurting one another. So we seldom settled anything after we argued. We just kissed and made up. The Lord in His grace helped us to refrain from ever having sexual relations before we were married, and we are thankful to Him for that. But we did make the same mistake many other young Christian couples make by getting too physical on occasion. There were times when it kept us from exploring each other's personalities more fully, getting to know each other on an intellectual and emotional level, and sharing with one another spiritually. While we did have profitable times of communication together, it was often easier to kiss and cuddle and forget the problems than to talk them through seriously and prayerfully.

It was a poor habit pattern that would carry over into our marriage.

WALKING TOGETHER

Sit down with your mate in the next day or two and talk about what drew you to each other.

"Could this be God's way of telling me Richard was not the one for me?"

5

MILES APART

The fall of 1950 found us two young lovers/fighters beginning four years of intermittent separation. I enrolled in Wheaton College, Illinois, and moved more than 800 miles from home, while Mary commuted daily from her home to Philadelphia College of the Bible, just 35 miles away. Letters were frequent for the first two years, and were filled with expressions of love and plans for the future. And we were together constantly during vacations.

But absence during the school years did not necessarily make the heart grow fonder. I began to have second thoughts about my feelings for Mary, and I finally decided that I wanted to pursue some other relationships at college. Meanwhile, Mary had decided that I was the one whom God had for her. She was approaching her third and final year in Bible school, and my decision to break up came as an unpleasant surprise to her.

"I remember feeling hurt and angry," she acknowledges. "I thought to myself, 'That dirty rat! How dare he do this to me. Why didn't he break off sooner?' By the third year in Bible school, couples had pretty well paired off and most of the neat guys had already been taken. Now what was I supposed to do? It didn't take long for the anger to subside and for me to realize that this could be God's way of telling me Richard was not the one for me. Maybe God wanted me on the foreign mission field, and maybe Richard would not be a missionary. But even though I had it resolved in my mind, the hurt lingered. It usually does. I decided to talk to one of my professors.

"Mr. Gordon Ceperley had known about my relationship with Richard for some time. Not only was he my teacher, but I considered him to be a counselor and friend. I told him my thoughts about the mission field. His advice was extremely helpful: 'Mary, don't go into the mission field on the rebound. If God wants you there, He will remove that love for Richard from your heart.' I accepted his advice and started to pray for God to remove the love if He wanted me to be a single missionary. My heart was sincere, and I really did not want to marry outside God's will. The pain continued, but there was a quiet confidence that a sovereign God would do what was best."

Meanwhile, I must admit that I was not being very successful in my other relationships. My dating plans at Wheaton were much more ambitious than my actual practice turned out to be. And by summer between my junior and senior years I was still very much unattached. My roommate, a childhood buddy, and I returned home to Bristol to work for the summer months. It seemed to me that he was beginning to put a move on Mary, and even though I had no claim on her, it bothered me to see him operate.

One summer evening the youth department at church had scheduled a party and nearly everyone in the group was there. Mary was being loud and boisterous that night, and acting most unlady-like. She now says,

"I wanted Richard to know that I didn't need him. If he didn't want me, then I sure didn't want him. Recently I looked back in my diary and read my account of the evening. It said, 'We had a big fight. He wants me to be a lady. Boy, that's hard.' "

I didn't like anything about Mary that night. I didn't like the way she was acting. I didn't like the way she was flirting with my roommate. I didn't like the dress she was wearing. As far as I was concerned, the whole evening was a confirmation of the decision I had made several months earlier. She was not the girl for me. And yet I had to admit that there was something in her that attracted me. I went home that night totally confused, and I asked God to give me clear direction for my life.

By morning my feelings had changed dramatically. I found that I wanted to be with her. It was a Saturday and I was planning to drive to Philadelphia to visit my mother who was in the hospital for surgery. Humanly speaking, I still cannot fully understand why I did it, but I called Mary on the telephone that morning and asked her if she would like to accompany me. She broke a date with my roommate (which I did not even know she had) in order to accept my invitation.

We had one of the most delightful days we had ever spent together in the six years we had dated. After the visit to the hospital, we had dinner together, then came to my parents' home where we listened to Christian records and talked about the Lord and our mutual desire to serve Him. By the time the evening was over, I had the guidance for which I had prayed. This was the girl God wanted me to have for my wife. Before the summer was over and I had returned to Wheaton, we were engaged to be married.

The biblical strategy for choosing a life partner is to seek God's will in prayer and then trust Him to lead. It never occurs to some Christian young people that God may want to guide them in this decision, so they pursue various relationships without ever consulting Him, and they let "chemistry" guide them rather than Christ. His Word says, ". . . in everything by prayer and supplication, with thanksgiving, let your requests be made known to God" (Philippians 4:6).

"Everything" would certainly include the person with whom you will spend the rest of your life. We made more than our share of mistakes through these years of courtship, but we did ask God to guide us in the matter of marriage. The confidence that He did guide us was one of the things that would sustain us when the going got rough.

WALKING TOGETHER

Acknowledge that God has made you one, and make a commitment to the Lord and to your mate that you will remain in this marriage and do everything you can with God's help to make it succeed.

How we almost ruined a great honeymoon.

6

THE TWO BECOME ONE

September 1953 to June 1954 was the longest ten-month period that either one of us had ever spent. We were only together for the Christmas and Easter holidays during that time, but both were memorable events. My Christmas present from Mary that year was one I would treasure for years to come. It was a reference Bible which I valued, but inside the flyleaf she had inscribed an obscure verse from the Old Testament that had become most meaningful to her: "Can two walk together except they be agreed?" (Amos 3:3) She was reminding me that we had agreed on our commitment to the Lord and to each other.

She says there was something else in her mind as well when she chose that verse:

"I also thought that once we were married, the disagreements and arguments which we had experienced through our courtship would work themselves out. I felt that marriage would be the panacea for all our problems. We walked the aisle with stars in our eyes on that sunny June day in 1954, knowing that God had brought us together and He would help us have a good marriage. One of the songs sung at the wedding was 'Savior Like a Shepherd Lead Us.' We chose it because the desire of our hearts was to be led by our Savior."

Several hours after the ceremony we were on our way to Niagara Falls, the honeymooner's paradise, and the first few days were ecstatic. But the habits people cultivate during their courtship do not necessarily change when they say "I do," not even when their heart's desire is to please the Lord. We were only several days into the honeymoon when some of our old habit patterns resumed.

It was a rather cool Canadian summer day as we set out to ride the cable car over the Niagara River rapids. We had only driven a few miles from the motel when Mary began complaining that she was cold. That was nothing new. She had been known to be cold when the temperature is in the nineties. But this time she had forgotten to bring her sweater. After discussing it for a few moments, we agreed to proceed to the falls rather than take the time to return for the sweater.

Then we saw the sign: "See the rapids, only 50 cents." So we paid our fifty cents each, which was a lot of money in those days, took the elevator as we were instructed to do, and were ushered out onto a wooden walkway along the river where we could stand and "see the rapids" (just as the sign had promised). It was a tourist trap. We wondered how many other unsuspecting people had been taken in by the deception.

We returned to our car angry that we had been cheated, and angry that we were not smart enough to notice that this was not the cable car ride we were looking for. We couldn't afford to waste even one dollar. This was to be a low-budget honeymoon. We had very little money, and we needed to preserve what we had for the imminent trip to Dallas and my enrollment into seminary.

A few miles down the road we came upon the attraction we had been looking for all along—a breathtaking cable car ride across the rapids to a cliff high on the opposite side. As we got out of the car, it became increasingly clear to me that it was too cool and windy for my cold-blooded wife. And besides, we could not afford another dollar. I suggested we forego the ride.

And the lid blew off! Mary began angrily accusing me of being inconsiderate and unloving. And the more she fussed and fumed and attacked my fragile self-esteem, the more stubborn I became. There was no way now that I was going to take her on that cable car.

As I look back on it, having learned a little more about acceptable communication, I realize that the argument was anything but inevitable. I was probably feeling irritated that she had forgotten her sweater. But if I had been thinking, I would have realized that keeping her warm on that cable car would have been fun! In addition, I was feeling defensive and sorry for myself when she attacked my character and doubted my love. But if I had been thinking of her rather than myself, I would have picked up the signals she was sending – that she was feeling unloved and of little value, not even worth fifty cents.

Had I been sensitive to her and accepting of her feelings, I would have said something like, "Honey, I think I'm still angry about being cheated out of that dollar, and that's why I'm reluctant to spend another one. I do love you very much, and if this is important to you, I want to do it." After all, this was our honeymoon, a once-in-a-lifetime happening. What is one dollar compared to the good memories of shared experiences?

Mary says, "I know now that asking Richard in a kind way would have been far more satisfactory than the accusations I made. Something like: 'Honey, this is something I really want to do. I realize it's a lot of money, but maybe we can make up for it by not spending as much for dinner tonight. Besides, you can keep me warm on that cable car!' "

It would also have helped if we both could have admitted our anger, then expressed a sense of humor over the tourist trap and the loss of our precious dollar. Something like, “Boy, they got us on that one. But we’ll be a little smarter next time.” A sense of humor is essential to good communication. Start asking yourself, “What is humorous in this situation? What can we laugh about together?” It will help to defuse the tension and draw you to each other in greater intimacy.

It should be obvious by this time that becoming one flesh does not guarantee harmony and agreement. Marriage is not the magic elixir that remedies all the ailments in a relationship. In fact, it usually intensifies the weaknesses that are already there, which we were just beginning to discover. And this was only round one.

WALKING TOGETHER

Rehearse one unpleasant incident in your marriage that could have been defused if you had seen the humor in it. Talk about how it could have been handled in a better way.

The honeymoon was over—in more ways than one!

7

BIG D

In spite of our big fight over fifty cents, we had shared some enjoyable experiences together at Niagara Falls. We laughed some—like when we visited the Cave of the Winds, a walking tour behind the falls. We looked so ridiculous soaking wet in those yellow raincoats and gray flannel booties. And there was the night we attended our first drive-in movie. When it was finished, I tried to drive away with the speaker still attached, and it cracked the car window. We were able to laugh about it, in spite of the anticipated cost of replacing it.

Getting to know each other physically and expressing our love for one another sexually was difficult at first, but we were able to work our way through it in a mutually gratifying way. Yet there was tension, and it seemed as though we were often on the verge of another argument.

But now our minds were on Dallas. After the honeymoon we had only a few days to sort through our wedding gifts and other belongings and decide what we would need for the next four years. Then we packed the car, and it was off to Texas. With no freeways, it meant forty-five hours on the road, a trip we made in three days. I did most of the driving, and Mary's responsibility was to read the map and keep me on the right track.

What I didn't realize was that everybody didn't know

how to read maps. When Mary got confused and gave me inaccurate information, I felt agitated. Although I tried not to show it, I could not hide my exasperation from her. I'm not sure what it was – maybe I would sigh, or roll my eyes. But something I did caused her to feel belittled. It was poor non-verbal communication, and it has sabotaged a harmonious relationship between us many times since.

Some students of communication say that most of us believe 93 percent of what we sense non-verbally and only 7 percent of what we hear spoken. Although my words were saying it was all right that she couldn't understand the map, the tone of my voice, or the look on my face, or something else I did was conveying a different message: "What's wrong with you, Mary? Can't you even tell me whether to turn left or right? Any idiot ought to be able to do that."

As you might suspect, she didn't respond very favorably to that. Her usual retort was something like, "If you don't like the way I do it, then do it yourself." But if I did stop the car to look at the map myself, she felt insulted and got even more angry.

We have both used poor non-verbal communication to hurt each other through the years of our marriage, and neither one of us fully understood the damage we were doing. We did it with the physical distance we put between us, with the posture of our bodies, with a raise of our eyebrows, with the shrug of our shoulders, with a frown, with the lack of a verbal response, even with the way we would turn and leave a room. There are literally thousands upon thousands of ways we can express disgust, disapproval and rejection non-verbally, and we continue to learn how important it is to be aware of what our body language is implying.

I have often interpreted Mary's disgusted look to mean she is angry and unhappy with me – when that may not be the case at all. She has often interpreted the unexpressive and disinterested look on my face to mean I don't care about her – when that is not true. We have discovered that, since we are not usually aware of what we communicate non-verbally, we need to help each other by explaining calmly what we sense in the other person and what we feel from each other. In the past, we usually failed to do that. We just assumed that we knew what the other intended to convey and we got angry about it.

As time went on, we also could have helped each other understand what kind of non-verbal communication would bring us affirmation and healing—like a hug, a touch on the hand or shoulder, a smile from across the room, or a twinkle in the eye that says "You're someone special." But we were not insightful enough to know that we should share those needs, and nobody ever taught us. Learning to communicate positively in non-verbal ways is a continual growing process. And we made very little progress in those early years. Episodes in the car on the way to Dallas were only one expression of our failure to encourage and support one another non-verbally.

In spite of our problems on the road, we did manage to arrive in Dallas without destroying one another. And now we were about to learn something of the cultural differences between North and South in the 1950s. When we tried to register at a motel for the night, the clerk questioned whether we were actually married, since we looked so young. When we went to a restaurant for breakfast in the morning, I ordered eggs, and much to our surprise the eggs were served with what looked like mashed potatoes. But they sure didn't taste like mashed potatoes! They turned out to be hominy grits, a new experience.

Another shocking discovery was the openness of segregation in the South. Things like separate drinking fountains for blacks and whites offended our sensibilities. And we found the Texas accent difficult to understand at times.

Interaction with native Texans, as well as with other seminary students from all over the country, made me keenly aware of accents. I had spent four years in the Midwest and had lost much of my distinctive northeastern twang. But Mary's accent was pronounced. And some of our new friends were making fun of her about it. That bothered me, so I determined to change Mary's accent.

When Mary was a small child she had a minor speech impediment and was never able to hear and reproduce sounds very accurately. She had always had a problem with proper pronunciation. In addition, English grammar and spelling were never her strongest subjects in school. All of these factors together were now becoming a concern to me. I wanted to help her learn to speak correctly for her own sake. At least that's what I said. But in my heart I have to admit now that I was probably embarrassed by her speech deficiencies. That evidently came through to her, and accounts for her resistance to my efforts to help her.

We would lie in bed together on Saturday mornings while I tried to teach her how to pronounce certain words. There were some sounds that she could not distinguish, but it was difficult for me to accept that when Mary tried to explain it to me.

She remembers it like this:

"I could feel him getting tense with me. I felt as though his acceptance of me depended on whether I could speak correctly, and I knew that he was displeased with me. I began to wonder why he ever married me in the first place. I did not feel his love.

"One day I jokingly mentioned to one of his professors that Richard was trying to help me lose my Philadelphia accent. He laughed. 'That's just you, Mary. And it's cute. Don't worry about it. Besides, that seems to be such a small and insignificant thing.' Naturally I told Richard what he said."

I needed to hear that. I don't think anyone had ever explained to me the meaning of unconditional love and acceptance. Somehow I had developed the notion that people had to perform in a certain way and live up to certain expectations before they could be fully loved and absolutely accepted. Mary had so many strong traits that overshadowed those weaknesses. But I was allowing the weaknesses to blind my eyes to her strengths. I wonder now whether picking at her speech was my subconscious attempt to strengthen my own self-esteem. If I could make her see her weaknesses, it would make me appear stronger.

But my prof's word of exhortation didn't help very much. I kept putting the pressure on her. There were other things about her that bothered me as well, and I was not hesitant to mention any of them. For example, she seemed to fidget a great deal—pick at her cuticles, bite her nails, chew ice. I coined a pet name for her that wasn't very flattering. I called her my little "idjit." That's a cross between an idiot and a fidget. I tried to say it in a joking way and claim that it was my own private, endearing term for her. But my smile didn't fool her for a minute. It hurt her, and it convinced her even more that my love for her was less than genuine. She responded as she might be expected to respond—by becoming more irritable and critical.

If non-verbal communication, accents, mispronunciation and pet names were putting stress on our infant marriage, what was to occur shortly would add even more pressure. God had a big surprise in store for us.

WALKING TOGETHER

Make a conscious decision to stop trying to change your mate. Instead of fretting over the traits you would like to see changed, suggest how they complement you, making the *two* of you a better *one.*

The doctor's news wreaked havoc with our careful financial plans.

8

ANOTHER MOUTH TO FEED

Before the wedding, we laid careful financial plans for getting through seminary. I was to work part-time wherever I could find a job, and Mary was to work full-time for Southwestern Bell. Since her graduation from Bible school, she had been working for Pennsylvania Bell and the company had offered to transfer her to Texas. So money would be no problem at all – with two salaries and low tuition at the school, we were confident that we could make it easily.

We had heard of the money struggles other married seminary students were having, but we were not going to have them. A shortage of money would never adversely affect our relationship. In fact, we planned to help some of our poorer friends with their bills.

Mary started work two days after our arrival in Dallas, and although I worked at several different low-paying temporary jobs through the summer, it was nearly four months before I found permanent part-time work. But after I was hired by the John E. Mitchell Company, a firm in Dallas owned by Christians who were sympathetic to the unique circumstances of seminary students, we were set. Or so we thought.

We were barely six months into our marriage when Mary went to the doctor for a minor ailment. She recounts the events of that day:

"I casually mentioned to the doctor in passing that my menstrual period was two weeks late. His examination revealed that I was pregnant. In the next few minutes I covered the whole gamut of emotions—surprise, happiness, perplexity, apprehension, fear. This was not in our plans. I would have to quit work. How would we pay our bills? What would Richard say? We thought we were being careful. Richard had even written a paper on birth control for a college sociology class on the family. His teacher had given him a *B*- and had written on his paper, 'Not practical.' He turned out to be prophetic.

"I left the office hurriedly since I was already late to meet Richard, who was to pick me up in front of the building. He pulled up as I reached the street, and before I opened the door of the car, I put my head through the open window and said, 'Guess what! I'm going to have a baby.' His first words were, 'You can't do that. You were going to help put me through school.' For a minute I thought he was going to drive off and leave me. I wanted to say, 'Hey, you were as much responsible for this as I was,' but I decided that standing in the middle of Live Oak Street was not the best place to argue about my pregnancy. It didn't take us long to get started after we arrived home, however."

Instead of accepting the truth that a sovereign God had this child in His eternal plan for our lives, we began to blame each other for what we viewed at the time to be a dreadful mistake. "If you had been more regular in using your diaphragm, this would never have happened." "Yes, but if you didn't want sex so much, I wouldn't have had to use it." There was so much more that was said, but all of it was designed to place responsibility for the situation on the other person. That too was becoming a way of life for us.

Mary knew that I was not very happy about the prospect of having a baby, and to admit any blame herself would have been to invite my displeasure with her. So she blamed me. And it was difficult for me to accept the blame for something I didn't think was all my fault. So to keep from getting blamed, I tried to lay the guilt back on her. Besides, it was usually important for me to win. Losing implied that I was not a very worthwhile person. I felt as though I had to insist that it was her fault.

It never occurred to me that fixing blame is a no-win exercise for everybody involved. It is a futile waste of time. It never solves the problem. It just keeps on intensifying the emotional level of the argument and driving people farther apart, destroying whatever closeness and intimacy may have existed. We both needed to know that it doesn't matter who is to blame. It doesn't matter who wins and who loses. All that matters is how we can strengthen our relationship with each other, and what God wants us to do next in this situation.

If we had thought about His sovereign control of all things, and His faithfulness in supplying every need, there would have been nothing for which to blame each other. Instead we would have been rejoicing together in anticipating this child, and looking forward to how God would supply our needs.

So many marital problems could be avoided if Christian couples would recognize the hand of God in every situation of life. The psalmist said, "Whatever the Lord pleases He does, in heaven and in earth, in the seas and in all deep places" (Psalm 135:6). And He never makes a mistake. "As for God, His way is perfect" (Psalm 18:30). He could have overruled our faulty birth control methods if He so chose, but He didn't. He had purposes and plans of which we were not yet aware, and all He wanted us to do was trust Him and rest in His infinite wisdom. We wouldn't have gotten upset with one another if we had acknowledged that God was in control of everything. We knew that truth with our minds, but we had not yet learned how to put it into action in daily living.

But one thing was certain: The medical bills for the baby's birth would be no problem at all. He/she was due July 25, 1955, and our hospitalization insurance maternity benefits would become effective on July 15. We had ten days to spare. First babies seldom come early, so God's scheduling seemed to be perfect. Except that Mary started labor about 2:00 A.M. on July 10. I told her to go back to sleep because the baby couldn't come for five more days. She insisted that the little tyke had decided not to wait five more days. By 9:30 A.M. we were the parents of a healthy baby boy whom we named Stephen John. We were pleased with the baby but unhappy with God's timing.

We learned, however, that while God does not always meet our needs as we think He should, He always meets them. When the bill came in for both the hospital and the doctor, it totalled only $6. We couldn't believe our eyes. We later discovered that five years earlier, when Mary's mother had a hysterectomy and cancelled her maternity benefits, the insurance company had mistakenly put those benefits on Mary's policy, unbeknown to us. They were willing to pay us for their mistake.

But even that unusual event did not convince us that God would supply all our needs. Mary had to quit her job and now we had to live on my part-time salary. We let our lack of money get us uptight and we fussed with each other constantly about money. Yet the Lord kept right on supplying all our needs. One semester I went to the seminary accounting office to explain why I couldn't pay my bill and to seek an extension. They pulled my records from the file and told me that I didn't owe anything. An anonymous donor had covered it for me. To this day I have no idea who that was.

And that unwanted baby proved to be a great joy to us. Steve came to know and love our Savior, and today serves Him as a missionary in the country of Ethiopia. He and his delightful wife, Marcia, have presented us with our first grandchildren. We would have forfeited one of the great joys of our lives if God had allowed us to have our own way. His ways are truly perfect! And we are still learning that there is no need to argue, no need to blame. We can accept every circumstance from His gracious hand and trust Him to do what is best.

WALKING TOGETHER

Acknowledge that blaming one another is a no-win situation, that God is in control of your circumstances and will help you through them. Now suggest some ways in which that confidence can affect your attitudes and actions toward each other.

When we did *have time alone, it seemed as though we spent it arguing about trivialities.*

9

THE MONEY TRAP

The purpose for being at Dallas Theological Seminary was to prepare me to serve the Lord in whatever way He directed. I did not know how that would be as yet, but I wanted to be ready, so I poured myself into my studies. Every spare moment was spent on homework, papers and studying for exams. And since Mary was no longer working, except for a few baby-sitting jobs, I went to work every day after school and all day Saturday in order to support my family.

Time to spend with Mary was not very plentiful. And when we did have time alone, it seemed as though we spent it arguing about trivialities rather than enjoying one another's company.

We both remember good times with Steve and good times with our friends, but those arguments still linger in our minds. As we recall, many of them revolved around money. One part-time salary did not go very far, and Mary complained incessantly that we did not have enough to make ends meet. She was an outstanding manager, always finding the best buys and seldom wasting a penny. But in her mind that meant I should never spend *anything* on myself, not even for a bottle of pop to drink with my lunch at work. She would expect an accounting of everything, and would scold me if I had not lived up to her expectations. She felt as though I did not appreciate her efforts to balance the budget.

She remembers it like this:

"I did not only begrudge Richard the privilege of spending money on himself, but I was just as tough on myself. I figure that during the school year Richard brought home about $28 a week, and even in the early fifties that was not very much money. Eleven dollars of it went for rent each week, and at least $3 was given to the Lord's work. The remaining $14 had to cover food, gas, car repairs, medical bills, insurance, school fees, books, telephone and miscellaneous expenses. That didn't leave any to spend for personal wants. Maybe you can understand now why every dime was so very important to me.

"We were both agreed that the Lord's money would always come off the top, that we would pay our regular bills next, and that we would live on what was left. God honored that commitment. He kept extra expenses such as doctor's bills to a minimum, He enabled us to meet all of our obligations, He provided sales at just the right time, and He faithfully supplied all of our needs. When we finished our four years at Dallas Seminary we owed no one anything.

"As I look back on it now, I realize that it was wise and glorifying to the Lord for me to be careful with our money and not to spend it foolishly. It was prudent for us to learn to do without things we did not really need. But it was foolish and sinful for me to be anxious, upset and critical about it. We could have avoided many unpleasant arguments if I had believed God's promise to supply all our needs (Philippians 4:13), and taken the lack of money as a challenge to see how God would provide."

As I think back to my attitude during those struggles, I felt that I was trying to provide for my family and to cooperate with Mary to the best of my ability, so her accusations that I didn't appreciate her efforts to stretch the money were difficult for me to accept. But I was thankful to God for a wife who was frugal, and who refused to spend money without consulting both the Lord and me about it. She maintains those traits to this day, and I continue to be grateful for them.

We both find as a result of our counseling ministries that free and careless spenders bring a great deal of stress to a marriage relationship. Some complain about their spouses spending too freely, but think nothing of buying luxuries for themselves without talking to either the Lord or their mates about it. If we want to enjoy harmony in our marriages, we will need to agree with each other about how we should use our money, and both of us must live by the same rules. We will need to recognize that God supplies our money and that it all belongs to Him. He wants us to pray together, plan together, and agree on how He wants us to spend it.

We frequently observe differing priorities between husbands and wives in the way money should be spent. One spouse wants to save, the other wants to buy a new car or go on an expensive vacation. One wants to limit spending to necessities, the other wants to spend lavishly on luxuries. One wants to give to the Lord's work, the other finds excuses to keep from giving. We can only surmount obstacles such as these as we seek God's will together, communicate with one another with an open mind and a pliable spirit, prayerfully consider one another's opinions and willingly put the other person's welfare before our own.

Once we agree on how the money should be spent, we must *both* abide by the decision. Budgets may be helpful for some, but there will always be situations where exceptions must be made by mutual consent. The important thing is to live within our income and to be content with what God has allowed us to have.

We have also encountered marriages in which the husband has insisted that providing material things is the proof of his love. So he spends hours making the money to give his family possessions, while withholding from them his time, his love, his attention, or his interest in the activities that interest them. He cannot understand or accept the reality that his family wants him more than they want his money. If he refuses to listen to them and continues on the course he has chosen, the time will come when they despise him for it, when they really do want nothing from him but his paycheck. And by then it will be too late to salvage his relationship with either his wife or his children.

I never thought for a moment that money could replace my time with my family, but we were still caught in that money trap—worrying about how we would pay our bills, doubting that God would meet our needs, and squabbling over what we should or should not buy. It would continue after graduation and into my first pastorate where I earned less than $4000 per year. And in the pastorate those inevitable time pressures would increase, complicating the problems we were already experiencing.

WALKING TOGETHER

Are you caught in the money trap? Maybe you spend too freely, or else you are too frugal. Discuss your spending habits together, then decide how you are going to budget your money.

"The problem was me. I needed a change of attitude."

10

THE LIGHT BEGINS TO DAWN

As graduation neared, we faced a dilemma. Several professors were encouraging me to stay on for graduate study and work toward the doctor of theology degree. With no practical experience to speak of, I wanted to find a place of ministry along with the classroom work in order to keep me from stagnating spiritually. Mary agreed, and we began to pray together that God would open a pastorate near enough to the seminary to allow me to pursue doctoral work.

After a full year without a pastor, and frustrated at every turn in looking for an older and more experienced man, the Fort Worth Bible Church finally decided to consider a recent graduate. It would be less than an hour's drive from the seminary. I was one of three men recommended by the seminary, and for some unknown reason the church began the candidating process with me. They would vote after I had preached for two successive Sundays, and if I did not receive the necessary 75 percent majority, they would go on to the second candidate. Much to our delight, the church called me (with a fraction of a percentage point over what was required). And we began our pastoral ministry–young and green as we were.

Mary describes our new life like this:

"What I had looked forward to since I was a young girl was finally a reality. I was now a pastor's wife. For the first time we would have our own little home rather than a seminary apartment. And Richard would have more time for me, for Steve, and for the next little one who was due to arrive in six months.

"It didn't take long for my bubble to burst, however. The pressures on Richard were greater than ever. Now he was not only driving to Dallas two afternoons a week to attend classes, he was preaching Sunday mornings and evenings, teaching an adult Sunday school class, giving a devotional study at Wednesday night prayer service, marrying couples from the church, burying the dead, visiting prospects and hospital patients, counseling, attending board meetings, and doing all the other thing pastors do. In addition to that, the church was too small to hire a secretary, so he was typing the Sunday bulletins, printing them, folding them, and handling church mailings. He was hardly ever home. In fact, he was gone from home more than he had ever been during the previous four years.

"And I was left with the kids. And they kept coming. Mike arrived during our first half year in the pastorate. Ten and a half months later, Mark was born. Richard's dad jokingly quipped, 'I knew God said we were supposed to be fruitful and replenish the earth, but you two don't have to do it all by yourselves.'

"Money was still scarce, so I was minding another child during the day to help with expenses. Although as a teenager I had always loved children, there were times now when I was getting frustrated and exasperated having them under foot all the time. There were always diapers to be changed, noses to be wiped, formula to be made, clothes to be washed and ironed, meals to be prepared, discipline to be administered, battles to be refereed, and bedtime rituals to be followed.

"In Richard's defense, I should say that he was almost always home from five to seven in the evening. During that time he would help me with the dishes, since the boys were nowhere to be found at dishwashing time. That gave us a few minutes to talk. Then he would spend some time with the boys. But that wasn't enough to satisfy me. He would usually have some evening responsibility, and I would be left with the children again. Richard would come home after they were snugly tucked into bed. And then, as you might expect, he would often want to go to bed and have sex. I found myself getting increasingly resentful.

"During our seminary days I had not been an easy person to live with, but now it was getting worse. I was unhappy about almost everything. I criticized Richard for not being home and helping more, for not showing me more affection other than at bedtime, for not being more considerate, for not understanding my moods, for not listening to me, for not talking to me as much as I wanted him to, for not taking care of things around the house, and for numerous other things that neither one of us can remember anymore. I complained about my responsibilities, I fussed about our lack of money, and I was discontented about something or other most of the time.

"I didn't like what I was doing to Richard and the boys, and I didn't like myself. But I didn't know how to change it. It seemed as though it was out of control, like a raging fire.

"There were times when I actually thought about taking my life. But several things hindered me. For one thing, I was afraid that I would not be successful and I would have to say 'I'm sorry.' I hated to say 'I'm sorry.' Another was the thought that Richard would remarry and be happy with his new wife. The nasty part of me didn't want him to be happy. And when I thought about it seriously, I didn't really want to die. I wanted to be a better wife and mother, but I didn't know how."

As I look back to the unpleasantness of those years, I know I loved Mary to the best of my ability, but I just didn't know how to make her happy. God had been so good to us and we had so much to be thankful for, but it seemed to me that nothing I did satisfied her. It seemed as though we were arguing about something most of the time. There were occasions when she had to go out in the car to shop or run some errands, and I actually thought that it might be good if she never came back. It is difficult for me to admit this, but sometimes I wished she would run the car off an embankment or something. But the selfish part of me didn't want to lose my car!

I can remember coming home at night after a meeting or after visiting in someone's home, then lying in bed and arguing until two or three o'clock in the morning. I was usually defending myself against the latest accusation. There were nights that I literally laid in bed and wept over the shambles we were making of our marriage.

About those late-night arguments, Mary says: "I started most of them deliberately so I could have Richard's attention. At least he had to talk to me if we were arguing. One night in the middle of one of those silly quarrels he said, 'Mary, either we get this marriage straightened out, or I'm going to leave the ministry.'

"I felt as though a bomb exploded inside my head. I thought back to my childhood aspiration to be a pastor's wife, to my decision to yield my will to the Lord, to my desire to glorify the Lord whether by life or by death. It occurred to me that I was willing to go to the mission field and be eaten by cannibals, yet I was not willing to be the person God wanted me to be in this marriage. I had said that I wanted to do God's will, but I wasn't doing what I already knew to be God's will. I felt like a liar and a hypocrite.

"God's Word says that I should be content (Hebrews 13:5). I wasn't content with anything. God's Word says that I should do all things without grumbling or complaining (Philippians 2:14). I didn't do much of anything without grumbling or complaining. God's Word says that I should rejoice in the Lord always (Philippians 4:4). I hardly knew what it meant to rejoice. God's Word says that I should live peaceably with all people (Romans 12:18). I was deliberately agitating my husband into arguments. God's Word says I should look out for the interests of others before my own (Philippians 2:4). I seldom thought about anything except what was best for me. God's Word says that I should be a helper to my husband (Genesis 2:18). Instead, I was hindering him. God's Word says that I should not worry about anything (Philippians 4:6). I worried about nearly everything.

"The light was beginning to dawn. I think I realized for the first time that the problem was not Richard, not the children, not the lack of money, not my tedious responsibilities, not the pressures of the church. The problem was me. I needed a change of attitude. I needed to begin obeying the truth of God's Word that I knew with my mind but was not as yet translating into life."

In our counseling opportunities, we both listen as the victims of unhappy marriages describe their plight. We wish we could magically transform their spouses into the people they want them to be.

But none of us can change other people. We can only change ourselves. What we usually do in those situations is encourage the counselees to become what God wants them to be. We each must appropriate God's grace and power to make the necessary changes in our own lives regardless of what our mates do. God may use the changes in our lives to affect them, but we must leave that with Him.

Mary was ready to make some changes. She never told me what God was doing in her life or of the decision that was crystalizing in her mind. And the progress would be so slow that I would barely notice it for some time to come. But it was a beginning.

WALKING TOGETHER

Examine your life in light of the biblical principles mentioned in this chapter. Choose at least one of them and begin to obey it, consciously depending on God's presence and power.

It took me several years to recognize Mary's commitment to change.

11

SLOW BUT STEADY

When giving her testimony, Mary has often said that she was 95 percent of the problem in our marriage. I used to think that was true, but I'm not sure anymore.

One thing is certain—at least she was the first one to make a decision to change. Here is how she describes it:

"I desperately wanted to change. I wasn't sure where to begin, but I knew that God was aware of my heart's desire and that He was going to help me. I'm not sure why I didn't tell Richard my thoughts. Maybe it was because I was too proud and was afraid I would not be able to follow through successfully. There had been times in the past when I vowed to myself and to him that I would change but failed miserably to follow through, and I didn't want that to happen again.

"Maybe I was afraid that he would perceive my intentions as hollow promises, and that would drive us farther apart. Or that I would not be able to change fast enough to suit him, and that would create more tension. I wasn't even sure I wanted to admit to him all the ugliness that I was discovering inside of me. What if he rejected me? What would I do then? I decided to keep my decision to myself.

"But I felt like I was making progress. I endeavored to cultivate a better attitude toward Richard and the children, which I hoped would create in turn a more pleasant and positive atmosphere for us all. A more thankful spirit was one thing I worked on. When I washed the clothes, I would thank the Lord for the washing machine that made the task so much easier. As I folded and mended socks, I would thank the Lord for the healthy, strong feet that wore them. As I went to the grocery store, I would thank the Lord for the money we did have and the wisdom He gave me to make it stretch. When I vacuumed the carpets or made up the beds, I would thank the Lord for my good health and the ability to do that kind of work.

"Sometimes I thanked the Lord for the inquisitive minds of my boys that led them to ask continual questions or got them into endless messes. There were even times when I was thankful for the act of sex, and that was not easy for me to do. I was grateful for the pleasure and the release it provided, not only for Richard, but also for me.

"The days were becoming a little happier for me. My thoughts of suicide were subsiding, and I was beginning to see that there was hope. I don't remember noticing any changes in Richard during that period of time, and he has since revealed that he did not observe much difference in my outward behavior either. Not telling him of my desire to grow probably made it easier for me to slip back into my old habit patterns too frequently, and every slip would bring all the previous unpleasantness back to his mind. Maybe I had hurt him so deeply over the years, that he saw my reversions to a negative, critical spirit as a continuation of the same old thing. But in my heart I knew I was growing. It was slow but steady."

After six years of ministry in Fort Worth, God led us to a new ministry in Huntsville, Alabama. Huntsville was a growing community, one of the major centers for the National Aeronautics and Space Administration where the Saturn moon rocket was developed and tested, and it was attracting a growing number of aerospace engineers. I had finished my doctoral work by this time, and the people in the Huntsville church were looking for someone with my educational background to minister to them.

Financially, it was a good move for us. During the last few months of our ministry in Fort Worth, Mary had been cleaning the church in order to help out financially. The church had wanted to pay us more, but simply could not afford it. So when the janitor resigned, she had volunteered for the job. She would get up sometime between 5:00 A.M. and 5:30 A.M. and clean for a few hours while I took care of the boys. It was added pressure for her and she was glad it was over. The church in Huntsville offered to pay us an amount equal to both of our previous salaries. It was a wonderful financial relief.

There were other benefits to the move as well. The church in Huntsville was larger than our previous charge, so I was able to have a secretary. That relieved some of the pressures. There were more young couples in the church too, and the fellowship we enjoyed with them was enriching to both of us. The house we moved into was larger than our home in Fort Worth, and with our growing family we needed more space. You see, when we arrived to begin our new ministry, our fourth child was due within three months.

The birth of our son Tim was additional evidence that God was working in Mary's life. As she recalls it:

> "We had not planned on a fourth child, and I was convinced that God would not give us one unless it was a girl. Both of us had wanted a little girl to brighten our home and complete our family, and I was praying constantly and fervently that the baby would be a girl.
>
> "And yet in every prayer, I said 'Lord, no matter how much I beg You, don't give us a girl unless it is Your will. I want Your will more than I want a baby girl.' This may seem strange, but I knew it was a boy before I saw any more than the head emerge from the birth canal. Yet I was filled with

joy, knowing that God had given me the desire of my heart—His will over my own. I thought of Psalm 37:4: 'Delight yourself in the Lord; and He will give you the desires of your heart.'"

But even though God was working in Mary's life, my eyes were blinded to it. It was probably almost eight years before I was willing to recognize any significant improvement. The way it happened was, from my perspective, one of the most dramatic points in our marriage relationship.

WALKING TOGETHER

Do you have a thankful spirit? Instead of murmuring or complaining, start giving thanks in every situation that God allows in your life, whether you feel like it or not. As you step out in faith to obey, God will give you the ability to follow through.

Mary's approach forced me to think about my contribution to the unhappiness in our home.

12

THE BREAKTHROUGH

Students of the human personality tell us that most men find their greatest fulfillment in their jobs. And I was finding a great deal of satisfaction in mine. But it was more than just a job for me. I had a sense of partnership with the living God. Serving Him was pure pleasure.

While I had seen no visible increase in the church in Fort Worth, the church in Huntsville began to grow almost immediately after my arrival. People came to know Christ in a personal saving relationship. Sunday school and church attendance increased dramatically from what it had been. People from the congregation said that God was using the exposition of His Word from the pulpit to change their lives and their families. It was exciting, and I poured myself into it wholeheartedly.

During the six years of ministry in Texas I had begun to wonder whether God could ever use me in any significant way. Now I was beginning to see that He not only could, but He would! The apostle Paul's exclamation of praise to the Corinthians was taking on new meaning for me: "Now thanks be to God who always leads us in triumph in Christ, and makes manifest the fragrance of His knowledge by us in every place"

(2 Corinthians 2:14). I adopted it as my life's verse. I was seeing spiritual victories and triumphs in people's lives, and it was thrilling.

I only wished that I had been seeing greater victories in my own family. Things were going better. The conflicts were fewer and less intense, but they still occurred too frequently to satisfy me. I wanted a home where peace reigned supreme. I have always struggled with a tendency toward perfectionism, and I guess I wanted the perfect home. Differences of opinion were acceptable. We could work through them, or learn to live with them. But conflict was intolerable. I didn't want any of it. My desire was not very realistic, but I did not understand that at the time.

The way I had it figured, we had enjoyed about one good week per month through the years of our marriage. Mary was tense and irritable for the two weeks before her menstrual period, and she was not much better during the week of her period itself. But the following week was usually pleasant, and I wished every week could have been that good. I considered her nagging and complaining to be an inconvenience to me, and I didn't like to be inconvenienced. I rationalized my selfishness by insisting that she was hindering the effectiveness of my ministry by her complaining.

But I have to admit, the bad weeks were not quite as bad as they once had been. She didn't seem to be picking at me and scolding me quite as much as she once did. Yet every time she did, my thoughts were, *Here we go again. She's never going to change. This marriage is never going to get any better.* Unknown to me, those thoughts were being reflected in my attitudes and actions toward her, and she was interpreting them as a lack of acceptance and love. As much as we think we can hide attitudes like these, they manage to come out in subtle ways and further corrode a relationship. I too needed a change of attitude.

During our time in Alabama we decided to take a busload of young people to Word of Life Camp in Schroon Lake,

New York, for a week. Our youth pastor rode on the bus with the young people, and we followed in our station wagon, since we planned to separate from the group after the week at camp and enjoy a brief family vacation before returning home. While only one of our sons was old enough to be part of the youth group, the kids in the group had no objection to our three younger sons riding on the bus with them. That left Mary and me in the car alone, and able to communicate without interruption for the first time in months (maybe years).

At one point I remember her sliding across the seat close to me and putting her hand on my leg. That was unusual for her, but I liked it. Then she said in a kind and calm tone:

"Honey, I need you."

I pondered that for a moment, and then in typical male fashion I said, "Huh?"

She repeated it again: "I need you. I need your attention, I need your affection, I need to feel secure in your love, I need to know that after the Lord I'm first in your life; I need your support and help, I need you to listen to me and talk to me. I need you."

To this day, she has no idea what prompted her to put it like that. She had never said anything like that before, and she doesn't remember reading it anywhere. I have no doubt in my mind that God gave her those thoughts.

Up until then she had always approached me from the perspective of my weaknesses and deficiencies: "You never help me when I need you. You never think about my needs. You always put other people before me. You don't pay attention to me when we're out. You don't spend enough time with the kids. All you care about is my body, etc., etc., etc." They were attacks. In many cases they were judgments of my motives. And I did not consider them to be true, so I defended myself, and we argued about it.

But here she was approaching me from the perspective

of her own need, and it stopped me short. How could I defend myself against a statement of need? I couldn't tell her she didn't have those needs, or even that she shouldn't have them. Her approach forced me to think about my contribution to the unhappiness in our home.

I thought that I was probably a better husband than the overwhelming majority of the men out there. And Mary would have agreed with that assessment. But if she had needs that were not being met, then without her even saying so directly, it was reasonable to conclude that I was not meeting them. I had been studying and preaching on what the Scripture said about marriage. I knew that my responsibility was to love her as Christ loved the church (Ephesians 5:25). I had learned that love for her meant seeking her greatest good above my own, putting her needs and interests and well-being before my own, being willing to make any sacrifice for her benefit. I obviously was not doing that. And this was the first time I realized it to any significant degree.

As good a husband as I thought I was, it was obvious to me now that I was not all God wanted me to be. And I determined then and there that I would begin to lay hold of God's wisdom, His power and His grace to help me obey the Scriptures and become a man of God in my home. I wanted to grow.

Growth was slow, just as it had been with Mary. Unlearning poor habit patterns and replacing them with proper ones takes time. But God got through to me that day. The long and sometimes painful process of growing was begun.

WALKING TOGETHER

Decide that you will not let the past destroy the future. When thoughts like *Here we go again; this marriage is never going to get any better* come into your mind, replace them with positive thoughts like *It's been a long time since that negative trait has been expressed. Praise the Lord; we're making progress.*

Begin to approach your mate from the perspective of your own needs and desires rather than his/her faults and failures.

We were both now committed to bringing greater harmony and warmth to our marriage.

13

A NEW COMMITMENT

The one thing above all others that had kept our marriage together this long was the commitment we both had made to do the will of God as best as we could understand it. We knew God wanted our marriage to succeed, and so divorce was never really an option for either of us.

Sometimes we felt the way Ruth Graham is reported to have expressed it when she was asked if she ever thought about divorcing Billy. She answered with tongue in cheek, "Murder—yes; divorce—never!" While neither of us ever seriously contemplated murder, there had been times when death seemed like the only escape from our misery, because we were committed to stay together till death do us part.

However, commitment can be a tedious, teeth-clenching chore when there is no hope. And that is what it had been for both of us during much of our married life. But from that day in the car, things started to change, because there was a new hope born of the new dimension that had been added to our commitment. We were no longer committed only to stay together because that was what God wanted us to do—we were both committed to make the specific changes in our own lives that would bring greater harmony and warmth to our relationship.

Let me explain my new commitment. I began to see that my defensiveness and withdrawal were purely selfish acts. When Mary criticized me and scolded me unjustly, I had withdrawn from her emotionally and sulked, sometimes for days. I could rationalize it beautifully:

I've been hurt and I need time to heal.

My silence will let her know how much she has hurt me.

Since it was something I said that inspired her attack, I will avoid future unpleasant episodes by not saying anything more than I absolutely have to say in order to exist in this house with her.

She doesn't deserve my warm affection after the way she has treated me.

They all seemed like acceptable excuses to me at the time, but now I was beginning to see that none of them was valid. They were all aimed at protecting myself, meeting my own needs. God wanted me to be thinking more of her needs than my own.

If I had been practicing what I was preaching—finding my sense of worth in who I am in Christ, finding my fulfillment and satisfaction in Him, finding His grace to be truly sufficient for me—then I would have been drawing on His resources to meet my needs. And feeling good about myself would no longer have depended on Mary speaking kindly and respectfully to me; it would have depended on my eternal unchanging relationship with Jesus Christ. I might not have experienced pleasant feelings when she attacked me, but my feelings did not need to hinder me from making the right choices and doing the right things. With my needs met in the Lord, I would no longer need to withdraw into my shell of protection. I would be able to reach out to Mary and minister to her needs, even when she accused me falsely, nagged me mercilessly, or argued with me over trivial things. And that is what I was now committing myself to do.

I haven't always succeeded (I probably don't even need

to tell you that). But there has been growth. Mary still projects a negative and critical attitude to me periodically. And while my first impulse is to withdraw just as I have always done, it is taking me less time to begin thinking biblically: *She really does want to please the Lord in the way she acts, so something has happened to get her out of sorts right now. Maybe I have been thoughtless or inconsiderate in some way of which I am not aware, or quite possibly her mood has nothing at all to do with me.*

But in either case she needs my unconditional love and acceptance right now. She needs for me to show an interest in what she is feeling, then listen to her attentively and sympathetically. She needs me to put my arms around her and tell her how much she means to me. And ministering to her needs right now is far more important than licking my wounds.

When I have been able to follow through on my commitment, I have made an amazing and gratifying discovery. Ministering to her needs rather than my own has drawn us together into a more beautiful closeness and intimacy than we ever thought we could have enjoyed. I have since read it stated by other authors—intimacy in a marriage grows as we satisfy each other's needs. And it works both ways. When I sense that Mary is putting my needs before her own, it draws me to her in warmth and tenderness, a sense of harmony and oneness. And she describes the same feelings when I forget about myself and concentrate on ministering to her.

So I try to be more open in sharing my needs with her, without being manipulative and demanding. That is difficult for me to do because it exposes my weaknesses and leaves me vulnerable to her. There have been occasions when she has used my honesty against me, and she will probably do it again. But God doesn't want that to stop me. He promises that His grace will be sufficient to sustain me at those times.

But I also endeavor to be more sensitive to her needs, to discover them by listening more carefully to her, to try to understand her more fully—then to act for her benefit rather than my own. I find myself thinking more often, *How can I respond to her right now in a manner that will make her feel more secure in my love, rather than in a manner that will project my selfish hurt?* I have failed to do that on far too many occasions, and I shall continue to fail. But I know that is what God wants me to do, and I know that when I do it, we will continue to enjoy a progressively stronger and more intimate relationship. So, weak as I am, and fail as I shall, that is my commitment.

And Mary has known that. She says, "I never saw Richard as a hypocrite, preaching one thing but practicing another. I knew he wanted to live what he taught, that he wanted to be a man who honored the Lord. When he was in the pulpit he was not so much my husband as my pastor-teacher, and it was his preaching that God used to change my life."

WALKING TOGETHER

Spend about fifteen minutes in quiet meditation, asking the Lord to bring to your mind ways you can change that will add harmony and warmth to your relationship. Claim His promise of wisdom as you think about it (James 1:5).

"Many times during each day I must make the choice between being positive or negative . . . "

14

MY WAY

Hope in a marriage has a tendency to ebb and flow with the winds of circumstance. When we are getting along well with each other our hope is at high tide. When we are fussing with each other, we wonder whether we shall ever be able to make the marriage succeed. And there were still periods when, in spite of my new commitment, our hope was at low tide. Mary was experiencing the same struggle. She was saying to herself, *I don't want merely to exist in a miserable relationship until I die. Surely God doesn't want that either, does He? And if He does, then I'm not sure I want Him.*

But she did want Him. There was no question about it. And Scripture verses which she had learned came flooding back into her mind, verses that assured her that God did want her to have a joyful life. Jesus said, "I have come that they may have life, and that they may have it more abundantly" (John 10:10). "These things I have spoken unto you that My joy might remain in you, and that your joy may be full" (John 15:11).

"As far as I was concerned," she says, "those verses meant that God wanted me to have a good marriage, not just one that I should endure while I waited for one of us to die. He wanted our marriage to be fun and full of joy even as we worked through our difficulties. Hadn't the apostle James said, 'Count it all joy when you fall into various trials'? (James 1:3). I realized more and more that the Christian life as well as a Christian marriage can be joyful, and I committed myself to helping make ours happier.

"The number-one problem I had to work on in order to help make our marriage more joyful was my negative, critical nature. Many times I tried to justify it by thinking, *This is just the way I am and Richard will have to learn to adjust to it. He needs to learn how to deal with critical people anyway. He'll be stronger and more effective in his ministry for it.* But eventually I began to recognize that my critical spirit was sin, so I confessed it to God as such, and finally I was willing to admit it to Richard. I determined that with God's power I was going to change.

"It has been tough – a constant battle. Many times during each day I must make the choice between being positive or negative, to be judgmental or non-judgmental. Let me illustrate: I am quick and impulsive; Richard is slow and thoughtful. I want things done now. He usually has something he wants to finish before he does what I want him to do. If I think that he should return a telephone call or write a letter to someone, I want him to do it immediately – not after he finishes opening the mail or reading the newspaper. If I want him to hang a picture or do some other odd job around the house, I want him to do it on my timetable, even if it isn't done perfectly. I have a tendency to insist that he do things my way, and to criticize him irritably if he resists.

"I want him to agree with my point of view as well, to see things as I see them. It is difficult for me to accept his perspective when it is different from mine, to admit that he has the right to a different opinion from mine. I am quicker to notice the things with which I disagree than the things with which I agree, and quick to make a negative comment if I see the matter the least bit differently from the way he has expressed it.

"I don't even like it that he has different tastes from mine. For example, I don't care to eat breakfast. A piece of fruit or a small sweet roll may be tolerable, but nothing more. Richard, on the other hand, enjoys a full breakfast of bacon, eggs, potatoes and toast. For years that bothered me, and when we were on a trip together I would argue with him if he wanted to stop for breakfast. I couldn't understand why anybody would want to take the time or spend the money to eat breakfast. If we did stop, I managed to make his breakfast miserable for him.

"But I am slowly learning to appreciate Richard for who he is and what he thinks, and to allow him his way of doing things. I am beginning to acknowledge that my way may not be the only way, and (heaven forbid) may not even be the best way. It is a continual struggle, but I must make the right choice at the moment of temptation.

"In addition to admitting that my intolerant and judgmental attitude is sin, and recognizing that God's power can help me control it, I must use the will He gave me and choose to act as He wants me to act. He did not create me to be a robot. He gave me volition, and He left me with the decision to continue my negative outlook or to view life more positively. I want to claim His power to think positive thoughts and speak positive words, words that edify and encourage. I want to choose deliberately to put away my critical mindset.

"Just a few weeks ago Richard wanted to cut up a left-over baked potato and fry it as part of his breakfast. I found myself feeling agitated because I wanted to use it to prepare twice-baked potatoes for our dinner, and I made a few negative comments. But as I thought about it a little further, it occurred to me that I was making a big issue over a *very* small thing and that I had a choice to make – continue resisting him, or admit that my husband was more important to me than a warmed-over baked potato. I decided that he was.

"Sometimes (as you can see from the potato incident) I

slip back into the old patterns of criticizing him and arguing with him simply because he is different from me. But I find that when I choose correctly, I experience much more personal satisfaction, and you can be sure that my husband enjoys my company a great deal more."

WALKING TOGETHER

Acknowledge that your way is not the only way to do things, and that to argue incessantly over insignificant issues can do untold damage to your relationship. Try to look at your differences from your mate's point of view.

Memorize and meditate on Romans 12:18: "If possible, so far as it depends on you, be at peace with all men."

The 15 principles that will make your love last a lifetime.

15

DO I LOVE YOU?

It had been a long time coming—nearly fifteen years. But finally the Lord had gotten through to both of us and convinced us that we each needed to grow. He wanted us to enjoy a warm and intimate relationship that would display His love. But learning to love each other with God's kind of love would be a life-long project.

There was nothing wrong with the way we were originally attracted to each other. I saw in Mary a fascinating, fun-loving, outgoing, physically attractive person whom I enjoyed being with. Mary saw in me a steady, stable, disciplined person whom she could trust to provide her with companionship and security. But as with most young couples, neither of us understood the meaning of God's love. There was no better place to learn it than from the Scriptures.

The thirteenth chapter of 1 Corinthians is the most complete description of love found anywhere in the Bible, so we spent some time poring over it. It was not written primarily to teach husbands and wives how to love each other, but to help members of the local church get along better with each other in view of their differences of opinion over spiritual gifts. But wherever God's love is expressed, it should look like the model Paul presented in this chapter. That meant we would have to digest its principles thoroughly and apply them to our own lives scrupulously if we were to grow in our love for one another as we had pledged.

We still have a long way to grow, but here are some of the things that are evident in our relationship when we are expressing God's love to one another. We try to measure the quality of our love by this standard periodically. You may want to do the same.

1. Love suffers long

People who truly love are tolerant toward and accepting of one another even when they displease each other. Let's face it, none of us is perfect, and Mary and I still do stupid, careless and inconsiderate things that provoke, embarrass, inconvenience, slight or hurt each other.

When she does things like that to me, I may still withdraw and withhold my affection. Her reaction is still to strike back with angry words, and that too is probably an effort to hurt.

But when we are allowing the Lord to express His love through us, we each admit our hurts and our fears, and we share our needs and desires, but we do it graciously and kindly, all the while reaching out to one another to keep our relationship growing.

2. Love is kind

People who truly love are sensitive to each other's needs, and endeavor to meet them even when they do not feel like doing it. God's love is giving-and-serving love. It makes us look for ways to help, to do whatever needs to be done for one another's good . . . not always what *we* think needs to be done, but what the other person thinks should be done.

For example, most women like flowers and accept them from their husbands as expressions of love. But Mary couldn't care less about flowers because they die. Bringing her flowers doesn't necessarily say "I love you" to her. But encouraging her to share her feelings, listening to her intently, showing an interest in what she is doing, offering to help her, being willing to work on a project together with her (like this book)—those things say "I love you." When I am willing to use the language of love that she understands, I am being kind. And God's love is kind.

3. Love is not jealous

People who truly love give their mates "space" to develop their potential and find their fulfillment in life. We have observed couples in conflict because the wives decided they wanted to go back to school and get a degree. The husbands were upset because they were threatened by the potential of their wives making more money than they made, or by the new friendships they might develop and the acclaim they might receive.

We have likewise seen wives who were jealous over the time their husbands spent with friends, in recreational activities, or in church work (assuming it was not an inordinate amount of time that robbed their families of their presence). They were jealous because their husbands got to be with adults, a world infinitely more exciting to them than spending all their time with little children. But love is not possessively jealous. It gives space.

4. Love does not brag

People who truly love refrain from rehearsing their good traits, particularly when their mates are critical of them. Bragging in a marriage often assumes the guise of defensiveness. And as you already know, this is one of my major weaknesses.

When Mary accuses me of something, I want to prove to her how wrong she is, so I may list all the instances I can think of that counterbalance her charges. That is boasting. When our children were little, Mary said to me one day, "You never take me out anymore." So I named every place I had taken her during the past month.

I totally demolished her attack and won the argument, but I widened the gulf between us. She was feeling neglected, and had I been demonstrating God's kind of love I would have explored her feelings and then done something to relieve them, rather than defend myself against the accusations by boasting of the good things I had done. Love does not brag.

5. Love is not arrogant

People who truly love do not stubbornly insist that their way is best and demand that their mates give in to them. Arrogance, like boasting, can come in different sizes and shapes, but in a marriage it often erupts in the "I know best – we'll do it my way" stance. And as you already know, Mary admits that this is one of her major weaknesses.

"There are times," she says, "when I think Richard says something stupid, because it is not the way I would have said it. And I let him know in no uncertain terms, like 'Why did you ever say a dumb thing like that?' I realize now that I am putting him down in an arrogant fashion when I speak to him like that. If I were demonstrating God's kind of love, I would acknowledge the value of his point of view and admit that maybe I could be wrong."

6. Love does not act unbecomingly

People who truly love are considerate of their mates' feelings and courteous in their actions toward one another. Sarcasm is a way of life for some couples. They ridicule each other, belittle each other and trade jibes with a fury, whether they are alone or with friends. They may say it is all in fun, but it leaves wounds that will someday become festering sores.

Mary and I used to play games with a couple who would snip at each other throughout the evening. "That was a stupid move. Why did you do that?" the husband would ask. "I learned it from you. Where else?" the wife would retort. The snide remarks would fly back and forth throughout the evening. It was one symptom of their lack of genuine love for one another, and today they are no longer married to each other.

7. Love does not seek its own

People who truly love look out for their mates' best interests as much as their own. This is the essence of divine love—total unselfishness. The apostle Paul put it in words none of us can misunderstand: "Do not merely look out for your own personal interests, but also for the interests of others" (Philippians 2:4).

I can see us both growing in this regard, and it is rewarding. For example, there was a time when, on those rare occasions when we had the opportunity to go out for the evening, we would argue over where to have dinner. I like Mexican or Italian; Mary likes Chinese. If I felt like I had to give in to her, it was reluctantly at best, and it usually spoiled the good feelings between us for the rest of the evening. Now if we cannot make up our minds, it is usually because we're both trying to please the other. I'm saying, "Are you sure Mexican is all right with you tonight?" And she's saying, "Are you sure you wouldn't want something besides Chinese?" We are learning to love.

8. Love is not provoked

People who truly love control their anger when their mate displeases them. We are all human, and all humans feel anger periodically. But we only express our anger in destructive ways when we are looking to someone else to meet our needs rather than to the Lord.

Mary admits to struggling with anger: "When Richard did not meet my expectations I could pop off with angry, hostile words which I usually did not really mean, words like, 'I hate you!' It amazed me to think that he actually believed what I said. I had no idea how deeply my anger was hurting him. As I have learned to trust God to meet my needs in His own way, I have been able to express my anger more constructively, like 'Honey, I feel angry when you don't listen to me. It would help me so much if you would look at me and show an interest when I talk to you.' It amazes me how positively he reacts to that kind of approach."

9. Love does not take into account a wrong suffered

People who truly love forgive the wrongs their mates commit against them. They do not keep score, or store up memories of past wrongs, then drag them out to win a point at some future time. They put those wrongs away for good.

I have had a problem with this one. Unfortunately, my memory of wrongs suffered is longer than Mary's. One night Mary made some statement to me that brought back many of the hurts from past years, and I found myself rehashing them with her. "You'll never change," I charged. We realized as we talked it out that there were resentments inside of me that I had never resolved through forgiveness. When I realized how much I had been forgiven by God, I had no alternative but to forgive Mary for the things she had done, and then refuse to bring them up again. True love cannot be expressed otherwise.

10. Love does not rejoice in unrighteousness, but rejoices with the truth

The word *unrighteousness* may refer simply to misfortune. People who truly love do not take pleasure in their mates' disappointments or failures. That is where some husbands and wives get themselves into trouble. Like Sally, who resented her husband playing ball so much, and gloated when he sprained his ankle and had to quit the team. Or Jim, who resented the amount of time his wife spent with a special friend, and crowed about it when that friend and her husband had to move to another city. When we are expressing true love, we hurt when our mates hurt and rejoice when they rejoice.

11. Love bears all things

A better translation might be, "Love covers all things." People who truly love do not broadcast their mates' faults in order to put them in a poor light. That doesn't mean we will lie to keep the ones we love out of trouble, but it does mean we know when to keep our mouths shut.

A loving wife won't run home to mama and whine, "Do you know what he did to me today?" That was never a problem with us because we always lived thousands of miles from our parents and we never had the money to go that far, but many women face that temptation. A loving husband won't run to his best friend and tell him all the witchy things his wife does. That was not much of a temptation to us either. We were both too proud to tell anyone how many problems we were having. We may have been following this principle, but it was more out of selfishness than obedience. Now we try to live it because we are growing in our love for one another.

12. Love believes all things

People who truly love treat their mates with absolute trust. Some husbands and wives torment themselves with groundless suspicions. When Stan's wife goes out of the house, for example, he conjures up mental images of her being unfaithful. When she comes home he wants to know where she has been, how long she has stayed, to whom she has talked, and what she said. He even has a problem when she goes to see the doctor because he's sure the doctor is trying to come on to her. But love thinks the best; it gives the benefit of the doubt; it trusts. And treating our mates with trust will help them become more trustworthy.

13. Love hopes all things

People who truly love look forward to their relationship growing more meaningful and precious. They have hope. Hope is an attitude that happily anticipates the good. It isn't a blind optimism that denies the problems, but it does look beyond the problems to a sovereign Lord who can accomplish spectacular things.

When we are expressing Christ-like love we may pray something like, "Lord, I haven't seen as much growth in my mate as I would like to see and I am tempted to get discouraged. But I know You can work in his/her life in ways beyond my comprehension and I am going to trust You to do that. Meanwhile, I am going to keep working on the things in my own life that need to be changed and trust You to use my growth to encourage my mate to change." When love is functioning properly in our lives it dispels discouragement, despondency and despair. It begets hope.

14. Love endures all things

People who truly love do not allow their problems to rob them of their joy nor of their will to go on. While Mary and I have let our joy slip away at times because we got our eyes off the Lord and on each other's faults, our determination to go on has never wavered. We have said basically, "Problems may assault our marriage – money problems, sex problems, health problems, in-law problems, children problems, neighbor problems, or any other kind of problems. But we are not going to quit. We are going to continue growing into the people God wants us to be, and keep on keeping on." We would not be married today if it were not for that degree of determination. It was the one thing that kept us going through the difficult times.

15. Love never fails

People who truly love are unconditionally committed to their mates until one of them is placed in the Savior's arms. True love never fades, never withers, never dies, never runs out. We used to joke that we could never get a divorce since neither one of us would take the kids. That wasn't entirely true, of course, but it does reflect our firm decision that divorce would *never* be an option for us. We have been and continue to be committed to each other – unalterably and permanently committed – come what may. And that is one of the major factors that has brought us through the troubled times. If you have never made that unchangeable decision to stick with your marriage no matter what, we urge you to do it now.

We have tried to share honestly with you how we measure our love. Maybe you would like to measure yours. For our speaking engagements on this subject, Mary and I have developed a "Love Test" to help couples relate these fifteen principles to their marriages. May we suggest that you and your spouse each take the test that follows, then compare your answers. It should open the door to some honest communication, and expose the spots where your love for each other needs to be fine-tuned.

THE LOVE TEST

(Based on 1 Corinthians 13:4-8)

Rate yourself from 1 to 10 on each of the following elements of love (1 being weak and 10 being strong).

1. I am tolerant toward and accepting of my mate even when he/she displeases me (*patient,* verse 4).

   Rating _____

2. I am sensitive to my mate's needs and endeavor to meet them even when I do not feel like doing it (*kind,* verse 4).

   Rating _____

3. I give my mate "space" to develop his/her own potential and find his/her own fulfillment (*is not jealous,* verse 4).

   Rating _____

4. I refrain from rehearsing my good points when my mate is critical of me (*does not brag,* verse 4).

   Rating ____

5. I do not stubbornly insist that my way is best and demand that my mate give in to me (*is not arrogant,* verse 4).

   Rating ____

6. I am considerate of my mate's feelings and courteous in my actions toward him/her (*does not act unbecomingly,* verse 5).

   Rating ____

7. I endeavor to look out for my mate's best interests as much as my own (*does not seek its own,* verse 5).

   Rating ____

8. I control my anger when my mate displeases me (*is not provoked,* verse 5).

   Rating ____

9. I forgive and forget the wrongs my mate commits against me (*does not take into account a wrong suffered,* verse 5).

   Rating ____

10. I do not take pleasure in my mate's disappointments or failures (*does not rejoice in unrighteousness, but rejoices with the truth, verse 6).*

    Rating ____

11. I do not broadcast my mate's faults in order to put him/her in a poor light (*bears all things,* verse 7).

    Rating ____

12. I endeavor to treat my mate with absolute trust (*believes all things,* verse 7).

    Rating ____

13. I look forward to our relationship growing more meaningful and precious (*hopes all things,* verse 7).

    Rating ____

14. I do not allow our problems to rob me of my joy nor of my will to go on (*endures all things,* verse 7).

    Rating ____

15. I am totally and unconditionally committed to my mate until one of us is placed in the Savior's arms (*love never fails,* verse 8).

    Rating ____

TOTAL ____

0 - 50 Improvement urgent

51 - 100 Improvement desirable

101 - 150 Learning and growing; keep it up!

WALKING TOGETHER

Take the Love Test. Determine in your heart to love the way Christ wants you to love and will help you to love.

Now make a copy of the test and place it in some conspicuous place where you will be reminded daily of the Christ-like love. Make daily choices to be obedient in this area, depending on the Lord to give you the power to do it.

If Mary would only shape up I could love her more. She felt the same way about me.

16

IMPROVING THE SCORE

There have been times when I've thought to myself, *I could love Mary more if only she would stop scolding me so much, or if only she would be a little more contented and even-tempered.*

Mary has had similar thoughts, except that she would finish the sentence a little differently: *I could love Richard more if only he would be a little more considerate, or treat me as though I were more valuable to him.*

We had bought into the world's notion that our love for each other depended on how the other person performed. If I didn't love her as much as I should, then it was obviously her fault, not mine. And if she would only shape up, I could love her more. She felt the same way about me.

Slowly the words of our Lord Jesus began to penetrate our dulled senses: "This is My *commandment,* that you love one another" (John 15:12). Love is commanded of us. Like it is *our* responsibility! Like it is something we can just do if we so choose! Like we can do it *regardless* of what the other person does! There is no honest way I can say, "But I *can't* love her like I should." What I am really saying is, "But I *won't.*"

We have made up our minds that we can, and we will!

We can do all things through Christ who infuses us with His strength, and that includes growing in our love for one another. We are going to see to it that by His grace and by His power our Love Test score improves regularly. And here are some of the practical things we do to help our love grow.

We think about each other's positive traits. When our love began to cool in those earlier years, we had the tendency to finish off the job, to throw ice water on it by occupying our minds with all the things we didn't like about each other, and by feeling sorry for ourselves because we had to put up with all those undesirable traits. There were times when we were so consumed with the negatives that we could not see the positives, and that is guaranteed to be a love killer.

Now we try to let our minds linger instead on each other's strengths. We do slip back into our old habit patterns periodically, but other people often help us get our perspective refocused. People will sometimes tell me about a positive contact they have had with Mary and mention what a help she was to them. It will inevitably remind me of one of her strengths. Mary says, "Women who have worked with Richard have told me how he has respected their opinions, and that has helped me appreciate that trait in him." If you are having a difficult time focusing your mind on your mate's good traits, listen to what some of your friends are saying. They may be able to help you.

It might also help to think back to the good traits you observed in your mate before you married. I can remember counseling with a woman who talked for nearly an hour about her husband's faults. When I asked her to tell me about some of his strengths, she sat there silent for a long time, then honestly admitted that she could not think of even one good trait. When I asked her what had attracted her to him in the first place, she began to recall some of the good things she saw in him before they married. I suggested that she write those things down, then add to the list daily as she thought of other positive traits he possessed. It helped her begin to appreciate him a little more. And when she began to show her appreciation, he became a little more thoughtful of her.

And that leads naturally into the second thing we do to encourage growth in our love for each other: *We try to act in loving ways.* One of the most powerful truths we know in the realm of personality and human relationships is that our feelings are determined by our actions. If we want to feel loving toward each other, we need to do loving things, to act in loving ways, to saturate our minds with the fifteen characteristics of love in 1 Corinthians 13 and then depend on God's power to help us put them into practice.

I realize that what we are saying sounds like double talk. First we tell you how we try to improve our Love Test score, and then we say that we improve our score by improving our score. But that's a biblical principle. In the letter of our Lord Jesus to the church at Ephesus, He said, "But I have this against you, that you have left your first love. Remember therefore from where you are fallen, and repent and do the deeds you did at first" (Revelation 2:4,5). That exhortation has to do with our relationship with Christ, but the same principle operates on the human level as well. We ask ourselves: How did we act when we felt loving toward each other? What did we do? What was it that pleased our mates, that said "I love you" in the language he/she understood? Now we need to do those things again. As Jesus put it, "Do the deeds you did at first."

Something very interesting happens when we do that. For one thing, we begin to feel good about ourselves because we did what God wanted us to do. We always feel better when we know we have pleased Him. Second, we feel good about the results. Loving deeds usually elicit a grateful response, and we feel good about that response when it comes.

Do you see what is happening? Our good feelings are building a positive emotional attitude toward each other that replaces the old negative one, and that helps us to feel more loving toward one another again. Since we like what is happening and want to see more of it happen, we do more of the same. And that keeps our love growing.

Mary has been particularly aware of this in her life. She says, "There are lots of days when I just don't feel like being nice. I would much rather be grumpy and grouchy with Richard, and snap at him for little things. But I know I should speak pleasant words, in kind tones. So I choose to do it, asking the Lord to give me the strength to follow through. It's amazing how much better I feel toward him before the day is over."

A third thing that helps to build our love for each other is *spending time together*. We have learned through the years that it is easy for us to drift apart. I could get over-extended in my ministry, and Mary could get preoccupied with the children or with her friends, and we would lose the intimacy of our relationship. Sometimes we each get edgy and irritable about it without actually recognizing the reason why. It is essential for us to spend some time together every day and to keep our two worlds merged into one if we are to enjoy a warm and loving relationship.

Sometimes we will talk for awhile when I get home from the office at the end of the day. If that is not possible, we try to lie together and talk about the events of the day before we drop off to sleep at night. Once in awhile we get away together alone for a few days, away from distractions, interruptions and responsibilities, and just enjoy each other. Such times are necessary for the renewal of our spirits and the rejuvenation of our love.

Mary admits, "There have been times when I have felt so distant from Richard and so involved in my own world that I did not even want to get away. I wanted to stay home and continue *my* lifestyle and not have to think about working on my relationship with him. When that happens to me now, unlike in the past, it usually doesn't take me long to remember what my priorities are to be. God wants me to put Richard and our marriage before my own wants, and when I do that, I find myself content and happy in the situation which I had been resisting."

One other practice has helped us increase our love level: *focusing our minds on the Lord*. The more I understand how much God loves me, the more it enables me to love Mary. The more I comprehend how much He has given to me in Christ, the more I want to give of myself to her. The better I grasp how much He has done for me, the more I want to do for her. The more I acknowledge how much He has forgiven me, the more I am willing to forgive her. And the more I simply think about Him, the more I want to be the husband He wants me to be.

As we study God's Word, the thing that He impresses upon our minds more and more these days is His ultimate purpose for our lives: to glorify Himself by making us more like His Son. As we allow Jesus Christ to control us and live His life through us, He reproduces His character in us. And His character is love.

The most important means by which our love for each other can continue to grow is for both of us to abide in Christ, to be aware of His presence in our lives moment by moment, and depend consciously on His power to make us into the people He wants us to be. As we get to know Him better and become more like Him, our Love Test scores are going to improve continuously!

WALKING TOGETHER

Having a happy and satisfying marriage takes time. Don't expect overnight changes. Just work on a few things at a time. The four suggestions in this chapter are worth your careful attention. Commit them to memory and begin to work on them. Remember that Satan is not pleased with your desire to have a successful marriage and he will do all he can to destroy it. Don't let him win this battle.

Finding the balance between two biblical principles.

17

IN-LAWS OR OUTLAWS?

"You think more of your folks than you do of me, don't you?"

"How can you say you love me when you side with them against me?"

"You're always ready to do what they want you to do, but you seldom want what I want."

"Why don't you ever cook _______ like my mother?"

"You sound just like your mother when you nag me like that."

"You let your parents run our lives. Why can't you stand up to them?"

We both came from fine Christian homes and had parents who wanted to do the will of God and who had no desire to interfere in our lives. They wanted only God's will for us—nothing more, nothing less. And as a result, we probably had far fewer problems over in-laws than most young couples have. Yet statements like some of those above were heard in our home periodically. So we need to comment on how we endeavored to work through the difficulties in this area of our marriage.

For one thing, we genuinely tried to practice the "leave

and cleave" principle. God said, "For this cause a man shall leave his father and his mother, and shall cleave to his wife" (Genesis 2:24). God's direction in our lives took us more than a thousand miles away from our parents' homes, and that forced us to weaken our parental ties and strengthen our bond to each other whether we understood God's command clearly or not. But the point is, knowingly or unknowingly, we did obey the exhortation of Scripture.

Many couples are not able to get geographically removed from their parents, and so it becomes more convenient for them to put their parents' wishes before their mate's. But the scriptural principle is unmistakable—after we marry, our mates come before our parents. Our parents are no longer in charge of our lives. There may be times when we need to make decisions that will be unpopular with them. While they may think they know what is best for us, that is not necessarily so. In Christian love we will listen to their opinions and consider them prayerfully, but in the end we must decide on the basis of what will be best for our spouses and our children. It may take a great deal of courage to stand up to our parents, but God will provide that courage if we turn to Him in faith. We must always act in love and kindness, but we may need to act decisively.

In the few spats we have had in this area, we each tried to point out to the other the influence we thought his/her parents were having. We didn't always do it in the right way. For example, "I feel belittled and unappreciated when you side with your folks against me as you did tonight," would probably have been better than, "If you think their way is so right, then why don't you just go back and live with them!" But however it was said, we each listened and tried to understand, and each tried to show the other he/she was first in our affections.

We had to remember also that we could no longer depend on our parents for material support. If they gave to us (which they did, generously), we would accept it gratefully. If they didn't, we would love and respect them just the same. But in neither case did we want to let the prospect of monetary assistance affect our decisions. We had to do what God desired and what was best for each other, and not allow ourselves to be manipulated by any thought of money. We have watched with sadness as some married couples have used their parents' money to control each other, and it has destroyed their relationship.

But there is another side to parent/in-law relationships that has become increasingly clear to us as time has passed, and that is the biblical exhortation to honor our fathers and mothers (Exodus 20:12). Some people have become so incensed over their mates' ties to their parents that they have demanded total isolation from them. They refuse to visit them, and they get upset when their mates visit. They try to keep their children away from them. If they are forced to be with them, they speak sharply and unkindly. We have observed that people who have done this have deeply regretted it in later years. How they wish they could go back and live those years over again!

Despite what some may think, our parents usually love us and our children and long to be a part of our lives. Even if they have a tendency to be overbearing or meddlesome, we have no right to deny them that privilege. Whatever their faults, they have a right to see their grandchildren, to be treated with respect and to be spoken to kindly. So be careful what you do, what you say and how you say it. Unpleasant memories sometimes linger for many years, much to everyone's dismay.

Most of the idiosyncrasies that upset us so are just not worth fussing about. When all is said and done, what difference does it make that your mother-in-law stacks the dishes in the dishwasher differently from the way you do it, or that your father-in-law likes to tell old war stories, or whatever? Love them and accept them for who they are, and God will bless you for it.

As the apostle Paul reminded us, honoring our fathers and mothers was the first command with a promise attached to it – "that it may be well with you, and that you may live long on the earth" (Ephesians 6:2,3). We would be wise to obey the command and enjoy the promise.

WALKING TOGETHER

Are your parents the reason for some of the conflict in your home? Apply the "leave and cleave" principle, endeavoring to balance it prayerfully with the "honor your father and mother" principle.

To me, it was always easier to play the silent martyr . . .

18

SPEAK UP!

If we were to choose the one area that has caused us more problems than any other, and continues to be our weakest link to this day, it would be the area of communication. And in that we are not alone. Many other couples echo the same frustration over their need to communicate effectively.

My problem was simply that I didn't! I've always been a rather quiet person, not prone to reveal my thoughts readily, and it has been difficult for me to be open about what has been going on inside of me. Mary would ask, "What are you thinking?" And I would answer, "Oh, nothing important." In some instances, I was ashamed to admit what I was thinking. It may have been a doubt or a fear, and I didn't want to admit it because it would have made me look weak. It may have been a wild dream, and I didn't want to disclose it because I thought she would ridicule it and make me feel bad. It may have been a lustful thought, and I didn't want to acknowledge that because it would expose my lack of spirituality. It may have been an angry thought about something she did that bothered me, and I didn't want to say anything about it because it was petty and childish for me to be angry over such a small thing, or because it might have instigated an argument which I would rather have avoided.

It was safer to play the silent martyr role. And besides,

that would make her suffer a little for hurting me.

Mary's problem was just the opposite, as she puts it:

"I blurted out almost everything that came into my mind, regardless of how it might have affected Richard. If I were angry about something, I seldom kept it a secret. I felt as though I had been taken advantage of or neglected in some way, I felt no hesitancy about letting it be known. Richard never had to guess what I was feeling. I told him in no uncertain terms, sometimes in loud, angry, insulting and belittling tones."

Neither of us was thinking about the other. We were each concerned about ourselves. Mary's attack would send me deeper into my shell for protection. And the more I retreated, the more forcefully she would come on, desperately seeking to have her needs met and desperately seeking to be understood. We knew that if our marriage was ever to improve, we had to work on our communication skills.

For openers, I knew I had to start talking, admitting what I was thinking, sharing what I was feeling, telling Mary what was happening in my life and letting her invade my world. So when I come home at the end of the day now, I try to sit down for twenty to thirty minutes and rehearse with her some of the events of the day, not only recounting the happenings themselves but also relating my feelings about them. For instance, if I have had the opportunity to introduce someone to Christ, I share the details and describe my joy over it. If I have done something poorly, I explain it honestly and admit my anguish over it.

When I am bothered by something Mary has said or done, I try to admit it instead of bottling it up and letting it build resentment. I endeavor to say it kindly and calmly, from the perspective of my own feelings rather than her faults, but I am beginning to speak up and say it. Not, "Will you please quit nagging me like that," but rather, "Hon, I'm feeling pressured right now. I would prefer to finish what I'm doing before I get started on that."

Honest communication does not mean that we must blurt out everything that comes into our minds. Some things are unmistakably hurtful and would be better left unsaid. But it does mean that we begin to develop a greater transparency about our thoughts and feelings, to share our hearts openly with the person with whom we have established this relationship of great trust.

How much should we tell? One good rule of thumb would be to share whatever affects our attitudes or actions toward our mates. If they are feeling the effects of it they have a right to know what it is. If I am feeling irritated with Mary because she has snapped at me, and my irritability is showing in any way (such as coolness, a sharp edge to my voice, a frown on my face), then she has a right to know, and I have an obligation to tell her—kindly and calmly and without laying blame on her, but honestly and forthrightly.

I have found that honestly admitting what is on my mind has helped make me more accountable to Mary, and this has helped me grow emotionally and spiritually. As I have grown, the pages of my mind have become more open still, contributing to a greater intimacy between us.

Mary is likewise growing in her ability to communicate constructively.

"I am learning that there is a right way and a wrong way to express myself," she says. "One of the most difficult things for me to do is to speak in a kind tone. I find that I get exasperated if Richard doesn't understand what I am trying to say, if he appears to be confused about what I am thinking, or if he questions me. I lose patience with him and reply in sharp, indignant or condescending tones.

"Sometimes I fail to express clearly what I want from him and why, and yet I expect him to know. If he fails to respond as I think he should, I find myself getting uptight with him and speaking in sarcastic or belittling tones. The same thing can sometimes happen when he doesn't agree with me or see things from my perspective. But I am learning that God wants me to speak in a kind manner no matter what I am feeling. I can say what I'm thinking or feeling, as long as I say it in love.

"I know now that I must allow him his own views. It isn't necessary for him to agree with me in order for me to feel understood. It's all right for us to disagree – to vote for different candidates, to have different opinions about how certain things should be done, to approach a passage of Scripture in different ways. I can express my thoughts and feelings, but to demand that he think and feel the same way I do is certainly not love. On the contrary, love is endeavoring to understand his point of view more accurately. The Lord brings two different people together to make a better ONE – to complete each other, not change or destroy each other."

One thing we have both found extremely important in communication is listening. It has always been easier for Mary to listen than for me. I have been the typical husband who often grunts "Uh-huh" to my wife when she is talking, while my mind is miles or decades away. And my interruptions with irrelevant comments have too often given me away.

I have learned that giving Mary my full attention is an important expression of my love for her. It doesn't come easy for me. It is an art that must be learned and cultivated. But I'm making progress. I've discovered that I cannot communicate effectively with the TV on or with a newspaper, book or magazine open in my hands. I must turn it off, lay it down, look Mary straight in the eye and say something like, "Let's talk about that. What you think is important to me. I really do care about how you feel." It makes me feel like a king when she shows that same degree of interest in what I want to say. And as we open up, share our souls with each other, then listen to each other eagerly, we are drawn together in an exciting and mutually satisfying intimacy.

WALKING TOGETHER

Good communication takes a great deal of practice. Set aside a period of time each day (ten minutes minimum to start) to listen to one another, asking questions that will help to clarify meanings and enhance understanding.

How to work through your disagreements and resolve conflicts.

19

THE LOVE FIGHT

It wasn't a happy evening. From the moment I walked through the door I knew that Mary was in an irritable mood.

I didn't know whether the kids had gotten to her, or some church member said something unkind to her, or some appliance in the kitchen wasn't working, or she wasn't feeling well, or it was "just that time of the month." But I suspected that sooner or later she might turn her wrath on me. I hadn't had a particularly pleasant day myself and wasn't about to look for trouble by probing for the problem. I just ignored it.

We got through dinner and cleaned up the kitchen, and I sat down to read the newspaper. Then it started. "You're not going to read that paper, are you?"

"Well, yes. Why shouldn't I?"

"If you have time to read the paper, then you have time to bathe the kids and put them to bed."

"Mary, I've had a tough day, and I have to leave for a board meeting in forty-five minutes. Let me relax for a few minutes."

"That's the trouble with you. You don't think about anybody but yourself. You just want me to do all the work, not bug you about anything, keep my mouth shut, be sweet all the time, and then be ready for you when you come to bed at night. You don't care about me or my feelings one bit."

I had suspected this would happen, but I still wasn't ready for it. I could feel myself getting tense and defensive, and my response was less than understanding. We argued until I left for the meeting. And when I returned home, the atmosphere was sullen and silent.

Now we were lying in bed, side by side, six inches apart physically, and yet hundreds of miles apart emotionally, both bodies stiff like two Egyptian mummies. Neither one dared to move an arm or leg lest it accidentally touch the other and be interpreted as a desire to talk it out, or—horror of horrors—to apologize. Thoughts raced through our minds—some real zingers that would score us some points in the contest, or maybe a conciliatory word that might open the door to restoring harmony between us. But neither one ventured a comment. We were in for another long night of conflict.

Must there be conflict like that in marriage? Why do two people who profess to love each other have to quarrel with one another? Can't two reasonably intelligent and mature adults live together in peace?

Yes, they can. There will always be differences of opinion. No two normal people ever will agree on absolutely everything. But they can work through those inevitable disagreements and resolve their conflicts.

How?

Some people simply withdraw. They think the best way to solve a problem is to run from it. But that doesn't solve anything. It just builds a wall between them, as I can sadly testify.

Other people fight to win. They won't quit until they've proven that they're right and their opponent is wrong, even if they have to destroy him in the process. But that just drives their mates farther away from them, as Mary can unhappily attest.

A third style is to yield. The person who always yields may think he is right, but it's not worth the hassle to prove it, so he just gives in and tries to forget the whole thing. But that builds resentment in him which is sure to come out one way or another.

A fourth method is to compromise, each one give a little and try to meet in the middle. Sometimes that is the only way, but it does carry with it the danger that neither mate will feel he has been completely understood or that his needs have been met.

The best way to resolve the conflict is to seek a solution that will satisfy the needs of both. Here are several things we try to do as we work toward that desirable goal. We want to turn our conflicts into love-fights that not only will resolve the conflict but actually increase our love for one another.

Adopt a learner's posture

Both of us will win in the end if we can both learn and grow through the experience. So we need to set that as our aim from the very beginning. Once we realize there is tension between us, the most important thing is not making the other person understand our point of view, convincing him/her that we are right, or winning the argument. Instead, the important thing is to learn something valuable that will help us become the people God wants us to be.

So if I really want to resolve this conflict, I will begin by saying to myself, *I need to break the silence (or stop running off at the mouth—whichever is needed at the moment), then reach out and begin to work toward strengthening our relationship, even if that means making myself vulnerable and ultimately making some changes in my life.* And since neither one of us has the natural inclination to do that, it will also help to pray, "Lord, help me to have a teachable spirit right now. Relieve me of my defensiveness, my self-righteousness, my anger and irritability, and help me learn something that will cause me to grow." If we can maintain that attitude, we're well on the way to resolving the conflict.

Listen with our hearts

My normal response is to show Mary how unreasonable she is acting, how wrong she is in her judgment, to talk back, correct her inaccuracies, refute her illogic, pick at details, explain why I spoke and acted as I did. But an inspired proverb says, "He whose ear listens to the life-giving reproof will dwell among the wise" (Proverbs 15:31). We will get to the root of the problem and work it out more readily if I will invite her to tell me what she is feeling, what her needs are, how she would have liked me to respond, and what I can do now to help resolve the problem in a way that will be best for her. My goal should be to listen attentively, to listen "with my eyes," and to understand not only her words but the feelings of her soul.

My hope is that she can share her thoughts with me without hurting me. But whatever she says, my goal should be to listen—without arguing, without answering back, without justifying my actions, without trying to get her to acknowledge my needs. My only comments at this point should be to agree, or to seek further clarification. If something sounds untrue or unfair, I should simply say, "What I hear you saying is . . . " and then reflect back to her my impression of what she said, then add, "Am I understanding you correctly?" At this point I must devote myself to listening.

Mary explains it from her vantage point.

"There are two things I would like from Richard—one is unconditional love as explained in the previous chapter, and the second is understanding. I want him to understand not only the meaning of the words I am saying, but what I really mean—the hidden meaning. I want him to try to feel with me, to be with me. I want to feel his support even when he does not agree with me. I don't want to feel put down when I don't see things his way. I want to be considered valuable to him.

"But if I want him to understand me, I have to make myself understandable. I must be willing to answer questions, to share my mind honestly, to avoid becoming defensive, to make myself vulnerable, to listen and think before I speak. And I must be willing to look at things from his viewpoint."

Keep our emotions under control

When we are falsely accused or misjudged, most of us get angry on the inside and reflect that anger in some way. We get intense, the frown on our brow deepens, the pitch of our voice rises, the volume gets louder, our tone gets sharp and has an irritable edge to it. And our spouses can feel our displeasure. Anger will never make a contribution to resolving a conflict and helping us grow, ". . . for the anger of man does not achieve the righteousness of God" (James 1:20). God wants us to put it away from us (Ephesians 4:31).

How? Not by bottling it up. If we do that it inevitably will come out in one way or another (either by an explosion or by physical symptoms). Not by directing it at ourselves (that is one of the major causes of depression). But by admitting it audibly ("I'm feeling angry right now"). Second, by identifying the reason ("I feel angry when you speak sharply to me like that"). Third, by forgiving the other for failing to meet our expectations. Anger is usually the result of frustrated wishes or expectations (yielding those expectations to God will help us forgive). And finally, by kindly expressing our needs and desires (it is important to let our mates know our wishes).

Ultimately we both must share what we are feeling, what we want, what we think we need, and why it is important to us. As we verbalize it, we may discover that it is selfish or childish and decide to drop it. But if we decide it is a valid desire and we want to pursue it, then we will continue to share it calmly, kindly, considerately and non-threateningly. If we can do that, the resolution is just around the corner.

Think before we speak

Some of us have our mouths in motion before our minds are in gear. And if we are trying to resolve a difference, that is like pouring gasoline on burning coals. Extended silence builds tension because we usually interpret it as disagreement. But some silence is good if we use it sparingly to think about what we want to say and how we should say it. Thinking before we speak will help us tell our mates what we are feeling and what we want from them without hurting them.

Most people have fairly fragile egos and prefer to be spoken to gently. Thinking before we speak will help us do that. "A gentle answer turns away wrath, but a harsh word stirs up anger" (Proverbs 15:1). We certainly don't want to stir up any more anger when we're trying to resolve a conflict. We want our words to calm and quiet, and that will take some forethought.

Focus on our own part of the blame

Our natural tendency is to blame each other: "You started it. If you hadn't said what you said (or done what you did, or looked at me with that condemning look, etc.), we would never have gotten into this fight." Blaming others usually stems from our own low self-image. We feel that we must win in order to establish our worth. Sometimes we blame others simply to avoid looking at ourselves and admitting what we have contributed to the problem. But that keeps us at arm's length from each other.

If we are serious about strengthening our relationship, we must ask ourselves, *What have* I *done to agitate this conflict?* If my partner feels hurt, slighted, neglected, unappreciated, offended, criticized, condemned, disapproved or rejected, then I must examine my own attitudes, words and actions. What have I done to contribute to those feelings? Even if I didn't mean to do it, the tone of my voice or the expression on my face may have fueled the feelings, and I must be willing to acknowledge that.

While Mary admits to starting the greatest percentage of the arguments we have experienced through the years, only more recently have I begun to realize how I have contributed to them, if by nothing more than a disapproving glance, or a probing question that subtly belittled her. Her hostile attacks would send me scurrying to my study (which was in our home) where I would sit and sulk and pity myself for long periods of time.

Once in a great while she will still come at me rather aggressively, and my first reaction is still to run to the safety of my study. But I no sooner close the door than the Lord begins to deal with me. I don't hear any voices, but the thoughts are surely there: *"What are you doing in here?"*

"I just came in here to get away from the verbal barrage, Lord."

"You need to go out there and admit your part of the blame."

"But, Lord, You heard what she said to me. That was totally unreasonable and untrue. It hurt. I need time to heal."

"Go out and admit your part of the blame."

Keep short accounts

It doesn't take several days to confront the issue anymore, usually just several minutes. And by that time, Mary usually has started to think about her part of the blame as well. And we are both ready to acknowledge our wrong, seek the other's forgiveness, embrace, and go on joyfully and harmoniously.

As the years have progressed, I have been called on to do more and more traveling as a part of my ministry and good-byes have been an increasing part of our relationship. There have been times when we parted without resolving some conflict and the thought in my mind has been, *What if this were our last good-bye? Suppose something happened to one of us before we were reunited.* Could the other live with himself/herself? It would be extremely difficult. It is our desire to keep short accounts with each other, to resolve our conflicts quickly and completely in a manner that keeps our love for one another growing stronger.

WALKING TOGETHER

Conflict is inevitable, but it can be resolved. Memorize the six suggestions for conflict resolution, and use them the next time you find yourselves arguing. Develop a "tough hide" as you work through the conflict, not taking things personally as a put-down, but trying to look at the situation objectively.

"One thing that helped me was for Richard to tell me honestly about his needs."

20

SEX, SEX AND MORE SEX

Rare are the husband and wife who have not at times bounced unhappily over rocks in the road of marital lovemaking. It is an enigma that something so enjoyable should be the source of so much tension and conflict, yet many testify that it is, and we are among them. It would be good for you to hear this story from Mary's vantage point.

"Before we married, I was convinced that I was going to enjoy sex immensely. I would never tire of it. Maybe other couples would struggle in this area, but not us. Sex would be no problem for us! It took no longer than the first night of our honeymoon to discover that I was wrong.

"The first hurdle for me was that I was unable to consummate the sexual act immediately because of fear. Feelings of failure, frustration and hurt welled up within me, expressed outwardly by tears. Richard was patient, loving and gentle with me and within a few days we were able to say, 'Yes, we are truly one.' It was a rough beginning, but now that it was behind us everything was going to be all right—I thought.

"But to my amazement I found that I could tire of sex

quite easily, that often I just wanted to be held and kissed without having sex. I also found that my young husband never got tired of sex. At least that's the way it appeared to me. There were times when I thought I had married an animal, that no other man wanted sex as much as he did. I used to tell him that if sex were right and good, then God would make me want it as much as he did. And since I didn't want it that much, it must not be what God desired. That sounded so very logical to me. It was another stress point in a stress-filled relationship.

"I have since discovered that while some women desire sex more than their husbands, the majority feel much as I do, and their husbands much as Richard does. He turned out to be a perfectly normal man after all. But no one had instructed us about the differences between men and women before we married, and so we kept muddling along as best we could. But I knew sex was part of God's plan for marriage and an important part of a healthy marital relationship, and I knew I had to find a way to work through my problem.

"One thing that helped me was for Richard to tell me honestly about his needs, to explain to me his desire for my body, to show me in the Scripture God's viewpoint on sex. God actually instituted it all the way back in the garden of Eden. 'For this cause a man shall leave his father and his mother and shall cleave to his wife; and they shall become one flesh. And the man and his wife were both naked and were not ashamed' (Genesis 2:24,25).

"Solomon said, 'Let your fountain be blessed, and rejoice in the wife of your youth. As a loving hind and a graceful doe, let her breasts satisfy you at all times; be exhilarated always with her love' (Proverbs 5:18,19). The apostle Paul put it like this: 'Let the husband fulfill his duty to his wife, and likewise also the wife to her husband. The wife does not have authority over her own body, but the husband does; and likewise also the husband does not have authority over his own body, but the wife does. Stop depriving one another, except by agreement for a time that you may devote yourselves to prayer, and come together again lest Satan tempt you because of your lack of self-control' (1 Corinthians 7:3-5). The writer to the Hebrews added this note: 'Let marriage be held in honor among all, and let the marriage bed be undefiled; for fornicators and adulterers God will judge' (Hebrews 13:4).

"I did some serious thinking about these passages in God's Word and became convinced that sex was good, created by God even before Adam and Eve sinned, that it was perfectly proper for a husband to desire his wife's body—that our bodies actually did belong to each other. I realized that I had to set my mind on doing what I knew was right. It would be an act of obedience. I had to consider my husband and his needs before my own feelings. That's what the Lord wanted me to do. It occurred to me that I could be thankful for a husband who was willing to share his needs and desires with me, and who would help me work through some of my inhibitions with gentleness and understanding.

"I have come to see that the choices I make in this area of life are extremely important. I can choose to turn my husband down, which carries with it the danger of making him feel rejected, or I can choose to accept his love willingly and respond positively to a kiss or a hug, even if at that moment I do not feel like doing so.

"There have been times when I have hesitated to respond positively because I thought it would mean we had to jump right into bed. When I explained that to Richard, he understood and he endeavored to show me in a variety of ways that I was not just a sexual object, but that I was important to him as a person. He also tried to be more sensitive to my feelings and desires before approaching me sexually.

"But as hard as he has tried, the whole issue of our sexual relationship continues to be a learning and growing experience for me. There are still times when I have problems. But I start at the beginning again and remind myself that sex is good, that it comes from the Lord, that it is pleasing to Him for me to give my body to my husband, that I have a choice to make and that no one else can make it for me, but that the Lord will help me fulfill my responsibility as a wife when I step out by faith and obey Him.

"And I have made a surprising discovery. When I respond as I know the Lord desires, I usually find myself enjoying sex far more than I thought I would. Seeing God work in this way has been a fulfilling adventure. I have also discovered that sex benefits me physically. When I am uptight, it relieves the pressure I am experiencing. And sometimes it actually relieves the headaches. The excuse, 'I have a headache' has long since disappeared from our house. Now if I say that I have a headache, Richard knows that I am suggesting that I want to make love."

That's a summary of our story about sex through Mary's eyes. It has not been particularly easy for her to tell it, nor for me to agree to her telling it. But we tell it for one reason only, and that is to encourage others who may be facing similar difficulties.

I would like to add a few comments from where I stand. I think my sexual expectations in marriage were much too high because of some literature I read from the world's distorted perspective before I was married. Men who consume the world's "fantasy" view of sex expect their wives to perform as the women in that unrealistic dream world, and they seldom do. When we stay with God's perspective and unselfishly seek to minister to our wives' sexual needs in ways that please them, rather than expect them to pleasure us in ways that they may find offensive, we will find ourselves enjoying true sexual fulfillment.

That is not to say that variety and experimentation in love-making are wrong. But it is to say that endeavoring to please our mates above ourselves results in sex at its best. And that is what we are discovering.

WALKING TOGETHER

God created sex and He said it was good. If it is a problem in your marriage, spend a quiet evening together talking about your sexual needs and desires, being careful to maintain an open and understanding spirit.

Headship means I can bark the orders and Mary must snap to it. Right? Not on your life!

21

CLARIFYING OUR ROLES

Some people would rather not hear about the roles of husbands and wives in marriage. They have been conditioned to think that there should be no distinction between men and women. But God made husbands and wives to be different, and He assigned them different functions in the marital relationship. We have found that our marriage works best when we understand our respective roles and fulfill them. Let us begin with the wife's role.

The Wife's Role

"While speaking at a women's retreat I was asked if I considered myself to be a submissive wife. Without a moment's hesitation, I said 'Yes.' After I heard myself say it, however, I thought it best to add, 'But that is something my husband could answer better than I. When I get home I'll ask him.' I remember thinking, *Of course Richard will say that I am a submissive wife.* But he didn't. And I didn't like that. So I decided to do a little study on the subject.

"I found that God called me to be a helper suitable to my husband (Genesis 2:18). Evidently he is not able to carry out God's plan for his life fully, nor become all that God wants him to be, without my help. And that puts me in a very important and strategic position. I have heard it likened to a golf caddy. He gives advice to the pro, carries the bag for him, and generally does all he can to enhance his game.

"And that's what I want to do for Richard. As a helpmeet I can give advice (so long as I do it in a courteous and considerate way). I can help to lighten his load by doing things for him—like taking the car for repairs, screening telephone calls when he is studying, running errands that will save him time, listening to someone's problem whom I can assist as capably as he, and doing other little jobs that will release him for his primary responsibilities of preaching and teaching God's Word.

"After the Lord I consider him to be my first priority. If I have a choice between two things, one which will benefit me and the other Richard, God wants me to do what will be most beneficial to him. I know what some of you are thinking—'But what about my needs?' I have thought that same thing at times. In fact, I still do. But the Scripture clearly instructs me to look out for the best interests of others as much as my own (Philippians 2:4), and that certainly includes my husband's.

"When my highest goal is to have my own needs met, I usually turn out to be a hindrance to him rather than a help. But when I choose to be a helper, God usually sees to it that my needs are adequately met. As his helper, I want to build him up and to encourage him, let him know that even when I don't agree with him, I will still love him, respect him and support him.

"But there is something else I learned about being a helper. Helpers are not in charge. And most wives need to be reminded of that. Maybe that's why there are so many references in the New Testament to wives developing a submissive spirit. Helpers will express opinions, offer advice, contribute insights, encourage, support, and lend a hand by using their unique gifts and abilities. But in the end they will submit to the will of the people they help.

"The more I thought about that, the more I liked what it involved, and the more I wanted to become a submissive wife. You see, that doesn't mean I have to be a doormat. Scripture does not degrade women; it elevates them. Scripture assures me that I am special and valuable. A true helper is not someone to be stepped on, but someone who willingly commits himself/herself to another. Submission is listening to him share his heart with me and seeking to feel what he is feeling.

"But after we have heard and understood each other, submission for me is willingly going along with his decision—not grudgingly, but willingly and agreeably—if for no other reason than that God has commanded me to do it, and I want to obey Him. That doesn't make me feel as though I have been destroyed as a person. On the contrary, it makes me feel valuable because I have been listened to and understood, because my opinions have been prayerfully and carefully considered, and because Richard has taken the time to explain clearly the reasons for his decision.

"There is a sense of security and satisfaction in knowing that, before God, Richard has the final responsibility for the decision. The buck stops with him. He must answer to God for what we do. And that is by far the more demanding role. As I have learned to surrender to God's role for my life, I find that I am happier and more content. I experience joy in knowing that I am pleasing my husband and pleasing my God."

The Husband's Role

Well, if the buck stops with me, it looks as though I'm in charge here. Although that can be a frightening thought at times, that is what the Scripture says. The apostle Paul taught that the husband is the head of the wife as Christ is the head of the church (Ephesians 5:23). That means I can bark the orders and Mary must snap to it, that what I say goes regardless of what she thinks. Right? NOT ON YOUR LIFE! When we study the life of Christ we learn that headship for

Him meant unselfish service. Jesus practiced servant leadership, and in that He is our example (cf. Matthew 20:25-28).

True headship in a biblical sense is not so much the right to rule as it is the responsibility to serve. Men usually think of serving as the wife's role, but God says it is the husband's. It is my obligation to look out for the well-being of my wife, to do what is best for her (whatever sacrifice that requires of me personally), to see that her needs are met and that things generally are taken care of for her.

I hear husbands using the concept of headship to get their own way: "You know what the Bible says – I'm supposed to be the head of this house and you're supposed to submit to me. And it's about time you learned it. So we'll do it my way whether you like it or not." That is the exact opposite of biblical headship. True servant leadership would sound more like, "Please tell me how you feel about this decision. I value your opinion and advice. What would be best for you? How will your needs best be met? Let's talk about it and pray about it together. I would rather not make a decision until we can agree."

I failed to grasp that truth for many years. But I find now that when I practice headship in this biblical sense, Mary finds it much easier to be submissive. She finds herself wanting to give of herself to me, to consider my desires and minister to my needs.

The one word that best sums up the biblical function of the head is *love*. "Husbands, love your wives as Christ also loved the church and gave Himself up for her" (Ephesians 5:25). In other words, He sacrificed Himself for our good, even while we were sinners. Many of us men are willing to make some sacrifices while we are courting, but once we have made the trip to the altar and completed the conquest, we have little reason to make any more. We're willing to show love to our wives as long as it isn't too inconvenient, or doesn't cost us too much in terms of money or time, or as long as they are being nice to us. We're willing to show love on our terms. But please, no sacrifices!

I'm learning slowly that true Christ-like love means being willing to give of myself sacrificially to Mary. Giving to her may mean expressing my love for her in the ways that she wants to be loved, not necessarily as I think she should be loved. For instance, she would rather have me do something nice for her for no apparent reason than just on the expected special occasions. Or when we are lying in bed at night, she often wants me simply to hold her without always trying to make love. That says "I love you" in a language she can understand. She may want me to listen to her when I would rather read the newspaper or watch some sporting event on TV. God doesn't want her to be testing my love by making those kinds of demands on me. But He wants me to be ready and willing to give to her in those areas. They are small sacrifices to make compared to the volumes of love they communicate.

Love that gives for her good goes the extra mile to show her that she is the most important person in my life, a precious and valuable treasure given to me by God. That may mean listening with interest when she tells me about the events of her day. It may mean telling her how much I appreciate all the ways she tries to help me, or making sure she has some money she can spend on herself without giving any account of it, or not begrudging her time to spend with her friends.

Love that gives for her good is unconditional. I must admit that it is extremely difficult for me to express my love when Mary is irritable or critical. I want to show her by my non-verbal communication that she is making life unpleasant for me at the moment. But those are the very moments that she needs the reassurance of my love, so those are the moments I must turn to the Lord for wisdom and strength to love, as difficult as that is for me (and sometimes I actually do it!). That's how Christ loves the church. He keeps on expressing that love even when we are at our worst. And that's the model for husbands.

Love that gives is also willing to learn and grow. Some of us men feel as though we have nothing to learn, particularly from women. There have been times when I have implied that to Mary and she has said, "Why did you ever marry me if you don't have enough confidence in me to listen to my opinion?" It stopped me short. She would point out to me that I had accepted advice from some man, but when she had suggested the same thing months before I had ignored it. She was right, and I had no acceptable defense. True love will motivate us to listen eagerly to advice, accept it willingly and act accordingly.

Wait a minute! There's a hand on my shoulder. I think my wife wants to say something at this point.

"Let me interrupt here, please. What Richard has been saying is true, but he has grown. I cannot tell you exactly when it happened, but over the years he has made a complete 180-degree turnaround in this area. I would consider his teachable spirit to be one of his most outstanding attributes today. It is one of the things I love and admire most about him. He is willing to listen to me and learn from me. He asks me my opinions and seeks my advice. When he is preparing a message, he often will come out of his study and ask me if I have any thoughts to contribute on the subject.

"Do you have any idea what that does for me? I feel ten feet tall (and that's going some, since I am only four feet eleven inches). I feel valuable. I feel loved. I feel like I complete him. It makes me want to meet his needs. It's amazing to me to see how his love for me increases my love for him. That is a scriptural principle: 'We love, because He first loved us' (1 John 4:19)."

Love is a choice. I may not always be feeling it, but I can still choose to act in loving ways. I don't even need to have the *desire* to do loving things. All I need to do is choose to obey the Lord, to depend on Him to help me demonstrate unconditional love in understandable and tangible ways. That is to be my major role in our marriage.

How It Works

One particular incident from our lives may help you understand how this submissive spirit and loving leadership works in a marriage. In early 1972, while pastoring in Huntsville, Alabama, I received a telephone call from the associate pastor of Emmanuel Faith Community Church in Escondido, California. He explained how the Lord had taken their pastor home to be with Himself and asked if I would be willing to come and preach for them some Sunday, with a view to becoming a candidate for the pastorate. They had received my name from several different sources and wanted to meet me.

The Lord made it possible for me to get away for a weekend, with the result that the church voted overwhelmingly to call us. And now we were faced with a very difficult decision, particularly since we were happy with our ministry in Huntsville and content to stay indefinitely. Although we began to talk and pray about the decision together, I set a day aside for prayer and fasting alone in a secluded cabin, and through my time of communion with God became convinced that He wanted us in Escondido. In one of the most dramatic experiences of my Christian life, God gave me specific answers to specific questions through a consecutive reading of the book of Isaiah, and I knew that we had to go.

As I made the forty-five-minute drive home that night, I remember praying, "Lord, it would be kind of you to seal this decision by having brought Mary to the same conclusion through the course of her day at home." I cared about her opinions and feelings, and wanted desperately for her to be one with me in this decision. I was anxious to get home and find out how God had answered my prayer. But I was in for an unpleasant surprise.

It was bedtime when I arrived, and as we got ready to turn in I asked, "Do you have any thoughts about our decision? What do you think we should do?"

Mary hesitated, then answered, "You're the one who has been fasting and praying all day. Maybe you should first tell me what you think."

I was insistent: "It's very important for me to hear what you have been thinking."

Finally she gave in. "Well, I was working around the kitchen today, thinking about the huge problem of moving all our belongings to California, and the thought came to me, *Forget it, Mary; you're not going.*"

As you can imagine, my heart sank. I felt as though God had let me down. Mary asked me what had happened in the cabin during the day, so I sat down on the bed and went through the sections from Isaiah with her. She was visibly moved, but non-committal. There was no resistance, nor argument—just silence.

We kissed goodnight, and she rolled over and dropped off to sleep. I laid awake for quite awhile, fussing with God for not answering my prayer as I had wanted Him to. And when I awoke the next morning, I was still out of sorts with Him.

I spent the morning in my study, finishing up some things I had wanted to do in the cabin the day before. At noon some of the men from Escondido called to find out if we had made a decision yet. I said, "No, not yet," and then I suggested the name of a friend of mine whom they might consider for the pastorate of their church.

During the afternoon I sat in our living room, reading the Bible, praying some more, seeking further light from God, and thinking that quite possibly my experience the day before might not have been of God at all.

Mary had chores to attend to during the afternoon—errands to run, chauffeuring of our boys around town for various activities, and so forth. But she would join me in the living room periodically to talk about the decision and to pray with me. My prayers seemed to go no farther than the ceiling. The Word seemed dry and meaningless.

It was nearly 5 P.M. when the thought came to me: *God showed you His will without question yesterday and now you are resisting Him and second-guessing Him. You must go. Be gentle and considerate as you tell Mary. But you must tell her. There is no other way.*

The next time she came into the room, I said, "Honey, please sit down with me. There is something I must say to you."

Her answer surprised me. "Before you do," she said, "let me tell you what the Lord has been doing in my heart this afternoon. As I've worked around the house and driven around town I've been praying, 'Lord, show me Your will. Lord, show me Your will.'

"Suddenly, a short while ago, it occurred to me that this was a different prayer from the one I had been praying for the last three months since the church in Escondido contacted us. All that time I had been praying, 'Lord, show Richard Your will.' But today I found myself praying, 'Lord, show me Your will.' It was then that I realized that the Lord had answered my prayer. He has shown you His will. And I'm ready to go with you."

The way has not always been perfectly smooth for us through these years, but neither of us has ever had a tinge of doubt about the place God wants us to serve Him. From the moment she expressed her willingness to support me in that decision, we have enjoyed perfect harmony over it, perfect peace in our hearts about it, and genuine joy serving Christ in the place of His choosing.

Your experience may never parallel ours exactly, but one thing is certain—where there is loving leadership from a husband and a submissive spirit in his wife, there will be harmony and peace and joy.

WALKING TOGETHER

Decide now that, by God's grace, you are going to do His will. Husband, choose to love your wife as Christ loves the church. Wife, choose to cultivate a submissive and respectful spirit toward your husband.

People often ask us how, in light of our problems, our boys ended up so well.

22

BUT WHAT ABOUT THE KIDS?

Whenever we have shared publicly the struggles in our marriage, one question that has usually come up is, "What effect did all those arguments have on your children, and how do you account for them turning out well?"

Actually, we tried to do most of our arguing away from the kids' hearing, but they obviously heard some of it. We've asked them what they remember and how it affected them, and we get varying answers. Some of it remains in their memory, but the Lord seems to have blotted most of it out. In chapter 24 they'll tell you what they remember and how it affected them. Here, Mary and I will try to answer the second part of the question: "Why are all four of them going on with the Lord thus far, and all four living productive Christian lives?"

Whenever that question is asked, we are quick to say that the final verdict is not yet in. Our fervent prayer is that they will continue to walk with God throughout their lifetimes, but only God knows whether they will. We certainly are not going to take anything for granted. But why are they living in His fellowship now in spite of our problems? That is another vivid evidence of God's marvelous grace. He saw fit to overrule our mistakes and put His hand on their lives in spite of us. In the final analysis, it is all of God's grace.

"But you must have done something right," people often counter. I think the Lord did teach us some things through the years that He used to contribute to their wholesome development. And we have helped each other as well. For example, I would have a tendency to demand perfection from them, to withhold my praise and commendation if their performance did not quite measure up to my standards. But Mary was extremely commending and affirming. She would show enthusiasm and excitement about the things they were doing and the little things that were happening in their lives. That helped balance my tendency to show disapproval, and it helped me learn to be more positive with them. But on the other hand, Mary would get angry and scream at them when they did things like fight with each other, or fail to make their beds or clean up their rooms. And my calmer temperament would have a tendency to balance out her more volatile nature and give them a sense of security and stability, the feeling that everything was going to be all right.

Here are some of the things we have learned and have tried to practice through the years, though sometimes falteringly. For one thing, *we have always tried to make the Lord and His Word an integral part of our home life.* We weren't always as regular with family devotions as we might have been, but when one of the boys would share good news with us, Mary particularly would usually say something like, "Wasn't it neat of the Lord to do that for you?" If it was bad news, usually we would suggest that we talk to the Lord about it and ask Him to work it out for the best.

If one of us lost something (like a contact lens—four of the six of us wore them), we would ask the Lord to help us find it if that would be best (since we were already on our knees, it was most convenient to pray). We wanted our boys to learn to consult the Lord about everything. And when decisions had to be made, we tried to share principles from

God's Word that would relate to those decisions. We tried to communicate the truth that the Lord Jesus is a real person who lives in our home with us and with whom we share all of life.

Second, *we tried to set a good example,* to be in the home what we were at church and before our Christian friends. We obviously didn't always succeed at doing that. But even when we weren't getting along, we tried not to pretend as though we were. Both of us despise hypocrisy and we wanted to avoid it at all cost. So we tried to be honest, to admit it when we were wrong, to apologize when we hurt someone, to be what we were asking our children to be. Some of the warmest and closest experiences I can remember with my sons were when I had to tell them I was sorry for misjudging them, or for treating them too harshly. They were most forgiving, but my willingness to admit my wrong helped to draw us together in a bond of love and respect.

Third, *we tried to make our family a high priority in our lives.* The demands of the pastoral ministry have always been great, but that time from 5 to 7 in the evening was practically sacrosanct. If I was counseling someone, I usually would tell him that my family was expecting me and politely excuse myself, unless, of course, it was an emergency. I tried never to schedule meetings during those hours. After dinner there was often time to throw a ball, play a game together, or wrestle on the living room floor. It was one of the things God used to cement our family together into a cohesive unit.

Fourth, largely due to Mary's influence, *we tried to guide by commendation rather than criticism.* Praise brings better results than put-downs. It helps to build a healthy self-image in our children, one of the best things we can do for them. Although we sometimes got upset when they spilled a glass of milk or broke a dish or a knick-knack, we tried to remember that those actions were unintentional and normal for children, that our children were far more important to us than any old dish. We wanted to let them be children and not expect adult behavior from them. If we had scolded them every time they tried to do something on their own, they eventually would have stopped trying to do anything, believing that they could not do anything right. Many adults have lived their whole lives through trying to overcome the low self-esteem they acquired in their families as they were growing up.

Fifth, *we tried to treat our children as people,* that is, to talk to them as we would talk to our friends, to accept them and appreciate them as individuals, to let them know we enjoyed having them around. They also knew that their friends were always welcome in our house, and would be treated kindly. We respected their privacy, particularly the privacy of their bedrooms. As they grew older, we knocked before we entered, and we did not rummage through their drawers.

We tried to listen to them and to understand their point of view, to see life from their perspective. We tried to include all of them in family discussions and let them be a part of family decisions. We learned that children are far more capable of handling family crises than most of us give them credit for. When Mary's dad was dying of cancer in our home, we all sat around in the evenings with him and talked freely together about death and heaven. Letting them be a part of that experience made a profound and positive impact on their lives.

Sixth, and it was one of our major goals, *we tried to prepare our children for independence.* From their earliest days, we let them do what they could for themselves. If as two- or three-year-olds they could push a chair over to the sink to get their own drink of water, we let them do it. We did not know it at the time, but we have since learned that encouraging independence in that way helps children become higher achievers. And all of our children have been relatively high achievers.

As they grew older we gave them as much freedom as they could handle. We let them make their own choices about things such as the clothes they wanted to wear, and we tried not to criticize them if their choices were different from what ours would have been. We tried to say "yes" rather than "no" as often as possible. We helped them learn how to handle various situations, how to act with proper manners around people, and how to make decisions for themselves. Our aim was to teach them how to live independently of us, but dependently on the Lord.

Finally, *we tried to maintain a sense of humor.* While we have to admit that we got upset too often, we also laughed a lot. Our boys remember times of fun around the dinner table in the evening, and those are some of their fondest memories. If we had it to do over, we would laugh even more and build more enjoyable experiences into their memory banks.

We were far from perfect parents. We made most all of the same mistakes that other parents have made. But we did pray a great deal for our children. We committed them to the Lord before they were born and asked Him to guide their lives for His glory. We are so very grateful to Him for His faithfulness in doing that.

Please – make your marriage work. You will be so glad you did.

23

A WORD FROM MARY

Maybe after reading this book you are thinking it is too difficult to work at your marriage. You are not sure you want to work that hard. You don't have the time. You don't have the energy. It may be easier to divorce, or even die. Maybe you are thinking that it worked for us but it won't work for you. Your mate is not teachable, not willing to work at improving the relationship. He/she will never change – what's the use of trying?

Let me assure you that I have had some of those same thoughts. In fact, there are still moments when I would rather give up. They are usually the moments when I think of myself rather than Richard, when I want to do things my way rather than God's way. I know the Scripture tells me to think of others more than myself, but I would rather not. How can I do it?

I have come to realize that I cannot do it in my own strength, but only in the strength which the Lord provides. When I am in a difficult situation, I must make a choice. I can fuss, murmur and complain, or I can turn to the Lord for strength, telling Him about my anger, frustration, physical or emotional exhaustion, then ask Him to work through me to accomplish His will. Then, I must simply choose to do the right thing. When I choose to do what is right, God's strength is there, enabling me to be obedient. But I must make the choice.

I must live one day at a time – actually one minute at a time – and not expect instant results. Improvement takes time, and I need to allow myself that time. I also need to work on one thing at a time and not get discouraged by trying to improve in every area at once.

I must also remind myself that God is a forgiving and longsuffering God. He does not give up on me, so I should not give up on myself. "And let us not lose heart in doing good, for in due time we shall reap if we do not grow weary" (Galatians 6:9). Life is short, and seventy to eighty years of unselfishness and sacrifice are nothing compared to the joys they will bring in eternity.

There are other benefits to perseverance in a marriage – the precious times together when we give thanks for a lesson we have learned, when we laugh over a shared memory, when we weep over a beloved friend who dies. And there are those moments of incomparable joy when we are surrounded by our children and grandchildren. Please don't throw your marriage away. Make it work. It will be worth it.

I do wish I could say that because we have written this book our marital problems are no more. That would not be true. In fact, we have had some struggles even as we have been writing. But that's all right. We are committed to each other, so we have been able to work through them. But more important, we are committed to the Lord and to doing His will.

I have changed over the years, and I know that I will continue to change as I come to the Lord, seeking to be more like Him. My prayer is for you and me to be aware of God's presence in our lives, to use His power to change, and to give Him the glory for all He has done and will do.

Our children think back on how the family held together.

24

REFLECTIONS OF FOUR SONS

From Steve, Our First

One of my earliest memories is of Mom vacuuming our bedroom in Fort Worth just before I went to sleep. I was in the bottom bunk and the crib was across the room (I imagine Mike was in it). I thought it was great fun to grab the vacuum and duck under the covers with it, but I knew if Mom was in a bad mood that was *not* the thing to do! So I would ask, whenever she was vacuuming there, "Mom, do you have a headache tonight?"

Another Fort Worth memory is of Dad's series on the kings of Israel and Judah. No, I don't remember any of the messages, Dad! But I do remember that that was the first time I paid attention to the sermon (I must have been seven or eight) and that was the first time it hit me what you did for a living and for a ministry. Watching you in the pulpit had a big influence later on me wanting a Bible-teaching ministry and career, so I would have to say that the series (one a seven-year-old could enjoy) began what would become an influence: your unhypocritical ministry of the Word.

I remember a few of our family fun outings as a young

child, like the excitement of going to Burger's Lake. I don't know why that place was so special, but it was! I remember the first trip to Six Flags. I remember looking for "Ready Kilowatt" on the road from Dallas to Fort Worth. I remember surprising Nanna and Grandad at their home for Christmas and the drive north (including the Christmas songs on the radio and Dad getting stopped for speeding).

I remember another, earlier trip when I was so thirsty I couldn't stand it. I don't know where we were going, but I do remember finally getting a drink! In fact, I have many memories of trips in the car. Maybe that's because the whole family was together (if so, that says something about the importance of the father being present to "make a memory") or because the vacation time was just a break from the routine.

Most of those memories are pleasant, except for the boredom in the car and you two getting mad at us because we were irritating each other in the back seat. More on that below. In later years I remember all the historical places we visited. I always enjoyed our family vacations together.

I remember Dad and me throwing the football in the back yard at Fort Worth. I would miss and Dad would say, "You need to say to yourself, 'I'm going to catch it, I'm going to catch it.' " And I would think that as Dad threw it again and, sure enough, I'd catch it. That was a good way to teach concentration, Dad! I try doing that with Mark now (my son)—though he's still a bit young. When it doesn't work he looks at me in disgust and says, "See, I knew I wouldn't catch it!"

I also remember us wrestling together, Dad. I think that was a good way to establish a healthy physical contact with your sons. You know, our family has never been a "kiss and hug" family. I think maybe a little more of that, especially with you, Mom, would have been good to teach the healthiness of certain kinds of physical affection.

The more I think, the more memories flood back, mostly later Fort Worth memories. I know you want more of the kind of memories that were to influence me later on, so let me share the one thing I remember about your own struggles as a couple. I remember occasional, loud exchanges between you and the feeling that you were angry with each other (this is all from Fort Worth days, now). I do remember not liking my feelings at the time.

I would say now that they were feelings of insecurity, but of course I couldn't identify them then. I don't ever remember fearing any specific outcome. For example, I don't remember fearing that one of you might leave the house and not come back or that one might hit the other. All I remember was not liking it.

You asked if they had any influence on me. Who knows?! I have had to struggle with insecurity many times in my life (even now, as a parent). Since I'm not a psychologist, I don't know how much of that stems from your struggles. But I imagine there was some impact on my later feelings of insecurity.

Another possible negative memory is of both of you losing your temper with us. I don't have frequent memories of that, but I do have definite ones! As I look back on it now, for Dad, it was when you perceived we had crossed the line (like when we'd be on a trip and getting onto each other in the back seat, and Dad would turn around, with his hand up in the air, threatening to swat one of us, and then turn back to face the road, then back to us, all the time with Mom saying, "If Dad has an accident, it will be you guys' fault." I laugh as I type this. That would be the ultimate guilt trip to lay on your children!).

For Mom I can't think of any specific times like that, but there definitely were times when I knew I had to tread lightly because you were right at the boiling point. Anyway, I do remember you both losing your temper with us. Mostly we had done something to deserve it, but in my mind you had crossed some line of control and I perceived you as out of patience and really angry.

I remember an incident in second grade when an old man on our road home from school got angry at me for walking through a roped-off area he had seeded for grass but which I thought was roped off so we *would* walk through it. I still remember the deep conviction I had of being wronged. I knew I had done what I thought was right. I remember telling you about it and you, Dad, getting really angry at the guy and you were going to go over and talk to him about it . . . until I told you about the area being roped off! You backed off pretty quick and told me just to not do it again.

But you did believe me when I told you that I had thought I was supposed to walk in that area. I had a couple of feelings from that incident: (1) You would stand up for me if I was wronged, so (2) I'd better be careful and tell you the truth because, in standing up for me, you'd find out about it sooner or later! and (3) you trusted me. When I told you I had honestly thought that was the right thing to do, you believed me.

I have many other memories of those earlier years (we moved from Fort Worth when I was eight-and-a-half), but none that I could identify as having a real "influence." So let me pursue later memories that influenced me.

From later years, the strong, formative things that happened in our home include the good times around the supper table with everyone cutting up. I think your presence, Dad, had a strong influence on that. Somehow we knew how to have fun and not cross the line into rowdiness when you were around. But now that I'm raising my own son, tell me, how did you keep discipline at the table and still breed that relaxed, free atmosphere? Another strong influence through early teens was Mom always being home and available right after school. I can't emphasize this strongly enough. It was very important to be able to sit on the bar stool in Huntsville, eat my afternoon snack, and talk to Mom about my day while she worked on supper. I think that is a major reason I learned to be a communicator with my wife; I learned to talk out my feelings with a woman right there. And Marcia thanks you for that, Mom. She says I'm more sensitive as a communicator than she is, and I attribute much of that to your availability during those teen years.

In this day of wives working and being less available to their children, you can drive that home hard! Women want a husband who communicates. Tell mothers that if they want to raise sons who will communicate with their wives, they need to be available to teach them how.

I have only a few memories of us playing sports together, Dad, after I reached teenage years. But your coming to my YMCA football games (and band events later on) and us watching and rooting for our teams on TV are strong memories. When you came to my games it let me know that you were interested in this important part of my life. Our watching games together gave us an area of shared interest during those teenage years when communication is so scarce.

I know I went through a period in the teenage years when I had a lot I didn't want to share with you, especially emerging sexual temptation and struggles, and dealing with periods of insecurity and peer pressure. Could you have done anything then or earlier to have helped me through that or made me more open about those things? I don't know. Dobson says all kids go through a time of cutting off their parents during teenage years, so maybe not. I felt like I got the "facts of life" stuff at the right time and in a healthy way. But maybe a weekend discussion when I was eleven or twelve as Dobson suggests would have better prepared me for the intense sexual temptation that a teenage boy faces, how to deal with it, and what God thinks about it. I'm thinking through those issues now since I'm wondering how I'll handle that with my own two sons.

(At this writing Steve and Marcia, with their three children, are missionaries in Ethiopia with SIM International.)

From Mike, Our Second

Almost all of my childhood memories are good memories. Growing up, I didn't know the things about my parents' rough marriage I know now, and which are written in this book. I'm sure that was good for me. Despite the fact that things were not perfect, Mom and Dad did a lot of things right. But first, you need to know a little about a few incidents in my life.

When I was only four years old I remember going to church and hearing the story of Jesus' resurrection. Even as a young child I knew that anyone who could rise from the dead must be special. I asked my mom about this and she explained who Jesus was and that I needed to ask Him into my heart in order to have my sins forgiven and go to heaven. I did that then. I continued going to church and memorizing Bible verses even though I didn't always want to. I'm so grateful now that I was forced to memorize, for most of the Scripture I still know was first learned in my childhood.

I respected my parents and always wanted to do things to make them proud of me. My older brother, Steve, was a good student, a good athlete, and as brothers go, a good brother. He set a good example for me and I tried to emulate him.

I never outwardly rebelled against my parents or against God. However, there were a few years in my early teens when peer pressure was tough and I wasn't really sure that all the religious stuff I had learned as a child was really true and worth holding onto as an adult. Inwardly I had an attitude which pushed God to the far recesses of my life.

I went to a Christian camp during high school and remember being touched by the realization that I didn't really know God as a close, personal friend. I knew about Him, but I didn't intimately know Him. I told God that if He were real, then I wanted to know Him like I knew my parents knew Him. God has been answering that prayer for over a decade now.

Now we get back to Mom and Dad. How is it that two

people who had such a rough marriage demonstrated to one of their kids that they really knew God in a way which would challenge him to one day pray that he wanted to know God as they did? First of all, they were not hypocrites. I knew that what Dad preached on Sunday he believed Monday through Saturday. God was a topic of conversation. We talked about what is right and wrong and why we should obey God. I watched as Mom and Dad not only talked about obedience, but did things to demonstrate obedience to God.

It's true that kids know when their parents are hypocrites. Mine practiced what they preached. I knew they weren't perfect. They don't even pretend to be perfect. But I knew that obedience to God was important to them and that they were trying to obey Him. They also gave us freedom and responsibility. I remember Mom telling me how freedoms given require that we take responsibility. Things were talked about and not just laid down as law. But when we broke the rules we knew that discipline would come. I'm told that I got more spankings than all my brothers put together. Underlying all the "rules" was the fact that we should get our direction from God and His Word.

I always felt secure at home. Mom and Dad may not have always felt love toward each other but I remember a lot of things they did which demonstrated love. I don't know if there is anything which can make a kid feel more secure than having a Mom and Dad who love each other. I don't ever remember seeing them fight. They must have done all their fighting in private. That was good. Dad was always home for dinner. It was nice to know we would all sit down for a meal at 5 o'clock when Dad got home. Consistency breeds security. Meals were fun. We laughed and joked as much as we ate (which was quite a feat for four growing boys). And Dad would always start the "basket shooting" at the end of the meal by wadding up his napkin and missing a shot into someone's glass. I don't know if we ever finished family devotions after dinner because someone would always make some joke which would be picked up by everyone else. But we knew that devotions were important even if we never finished them. We knew Mom and Dad cared that we were secure with them and in our relationship to God.

Last, we were encouraged a lot. Not just when we performed well, but just for who we were. I think that every time we went to someone's house on a social occasion, Mom would tell us on the way home, "You are good kids." I even told her once that she didn't have to tell us that anymore because we already knew it. It was nice to know we were accepted for who we were and not for what we did. In fact, that made me want to do things to make my parents proud and not do things which would be a bad reflection on them.

They say one of the main ways you get your ideas of what God is like is from your parents. Mine did a lot of things right. They kept the lines of communication open. They weren't hypocrites. They showed love and provided a sense of security. They let us laugh even at serious times. I think this is why I knew my parents knew God. I think this is why I prayed for God to make Himself real to me like I knew He was real to my parents.

(Mike has received his Ph.D. in elementary particle physics from UCLA and is currently involved in a post-doctoral program leading toward a teaching career.)

From Mark, Our Third

As a child growing up in the Strauss house, I would have to say that I was very much a follower. It would be a great understatement to say that my two older brothers, Steve and Mike, had strong personalities. Both were very influential on me and I generally looked to them for leadership.

Steve, the oldest, really ran the show. He would make up incredibly sophisticated and creative games which Mike and I would join in on. We always felt it was a great privilege to get to play with him and his friends. My real buddy growing up, however, was Mike. We were only ten-and-a-half months apart and I know I leaned and depended on him a great deal. We had abilities that complemented each other well and together we made a pretty good team.

One example of our complementary natures: We often would play football against two brothers who lived down the street. Even though individually they were both stronger, faster, and better athletes than either Mike or me, we never once lost to them. We just worked too well together as a team. This close tie and complementary abilities doesn't mean we didn't argue a lot, as most brothers do. But I would have to say we were very close, and I still feel a tie to him that is unique.

Because of such strong sibling influence, I cannot point to many *specific instances* of where I feel like my parents individually had a great deal of influence on me. Of course they did, as all parents do, but it is difficult for me to remember specific things. I think instead it was the family situation as a whole that was so strong an influence. I remember especially our times around the dinner table. It seems these were the most special times our family shared. The whole family enjoyed a great sense of humor and one hilarious comment would follow another. Most of us would be on the floor in stitches before the meal was over. I also fondly remember our family vacations. We would all pile into a station wagon stuffed from top to bottom with food and clothes and assorted junk, and would set off on our eighteen-hour driving days, jumping from one relative's house to another.

This emphasis on the whole family does not mean I do not remember anything about individual times with my parents. Positive things include times when Dad would take each of us boys individually out to lunch. I remember I considered it a very special thing when it was my turn. We would go to Shoney's Big Boy (a high class restaurant for us!) and talk together. That was a special time.

I would have to say, however, that I was probably closer

to my mom than my dad when I was growing up. I always got the impression that I was her favorite (I suppose all children do). Though my dad has always encouraged my strengths and abilities, it was Mom who was careful to point out those things that separated me from the other brothers. Whether it was "Mark knows people, let's find out what he thinks . . . " or, "Mark is creative, let's get his ideas," I always got the impression from Mom that I was "special" and had gifts and abilities that were different and unique from my other (highly talented) brothers. In the face of such strong sibling rivalry and talent, I'm sure this was a key factor in building my self-esteem. As I was growing up I *really* felt that I *did* know people better than my brothers, and that I *really was* more creative than my brothers, and that I *usually could* come up with the funniest statement at the dinner table that everyone would laugh at the most. It didn't so much matter that Steve was able to do just about anything to perfection, or that Mike's IQ was at the genius level, because I knew I was special.

I do not mean to imply by stressing my mother's influence that my father was not influential in this process, but I remember it more from my mom when I was younger. In my college and seminary days, I remember this same kind of encouragement from my dad as well. He would often say how proud he was of a particular accomplishment of mine, or just proud to have me as a son, and that was very special.

I think it was this encouragement that I was "different" in a special sense that gave me the family reputation later of being the maverick, or black sheep (in a family like ours, there has never really been a "black sheep," but I guess I was the most "off white" of the bunch). When I finally realized that I didn't have to do everything my brothers did, that I didn't have to like everything my brothers liked, I realized how *fun* it was to be different!

An example: I used to think I liked vanilla ice cream better than chocolate because Steve had always liked it better. Whenever I was asked what I wanted, of course I asked for vanilla, because that was *supposed* to be the best, everyone knew that (or at least Steve knew that, and he was *the* authority!). At some point in my life I suddenly realized, "Hey, I like chocolate, or even strawberry, more than vanilla!" What a shock that was! I was my own person. This realization of my own identity was quite a breakthrough and was especially important in a family like ours.

I now wanted to be different and often made an effort to show I was. I could play the devil's advocate in almost any conversation, taking the opposite side simply because the other person was so sure of himself. As I look back on my childhood, this was probably the most dramatic change that took place over my later developmental years. I went from an almost total follower to one who today finds it difficult to follow anyone or any cause without much skepticism. This skepticism and unwillingness to follow can have negative consequences, but I know in my case it did much to build my personal self-image.

As far as negative things from my parents, I think I was probably more sensitive to negative things than my brothers. I do remember my parents arguing and seeing my mother angry at us—things my brothers have said they do not remember much of. I also cried a lot when I was young. I remember trying to get through an entire year of early grade school without once crying in front of my classmates. That was an accomplishment! I remember particularly one instance in kindergarten. Whenever anyone had a birthday, they would get chocolate milk instead of plain old regular white milk. What I didn't know was that you were supposed to tell the teacher when it was your birthday so she could arrange for the milk. When my chocolate milk didn't arrive, I was heartbroken. A major trauma for a kindergartner! I guess it hurt to think I wasn't special enough to get this special treat on my birthday.

I also cried a lot in front of Mike, my constant source of support. I would lay on my bunkbed underneath Mike's at night and tell him my "problems" and cry. He would listen and encourage me that it wasn't as bad as I thought. What these traumatic "problems" could have been I don't even remember. But at the time they seemed very serious to me. I was also sensitive to things my parents and my brothers would say. I used to mispronounce a lot of words I had read and my brothers would laugh at me whenever I did this. It seemed they kept a running list of all the words I had ever mispronounced since I had started to speak (I probably mispronounced "dada") and whenever I made another blunder they would recite back to me all the words I had ever mispronounced, reliving the joy of making fun of me when I had said each one (I'm sure when they read this they will pull out their lists and have a ball!).

I remember, too, being very sensitive to anything I considered a negative statement from my dad. One I remember especially: I was having trouble sleeping and, hoping to receive some confirmation that I was "all right," I asked my dad if he ever had trouble sleeping. His response (as I remember it) was something to the effect that, "No, there is nothing spiritually wrong in my life that keeps me from sleeping." I was really hurt because I thought there must really be something wrong with me. I laugh now at how insignificant and mild his statement actually was (if, in fact, I even remember it right), and wonder how it could have hurt me. It really goes to show how much more devastating a parent's *cutting* or *abusive* remarks would be on a very sensitive child.

People have often asked me, "What did your parents do right in raising you that you all turned out so good?" At this point I usually deny that we turned out so good and start pointing out the numerous faults in my brothers (not really). I think two things were especially important. The first was family identity. We were a family and we all knew we belonged in that family and together we would make it. There was never any danger (that I knew of) that the family would fall apart. It was a special thing to be a part of our family and each of us individually were special. We had great times laughing and fighting and playing together.

The other thing is a real lack of hypocrisy. I, of course, never thought about this growing up, but as I look back I realize it. Many pastor's homes are full of hypocrisy because the father has to be the perfect and sinless pastor on Sunday, and he is a totally different person at home. This was not true of my father. He did not pretend to be someone he was not. Sure, people thought he was perfect (as some church members always will), but he never tried to give that impression himself. He was the same person at home that he was at church.

(Mark is currently studying toward a Ph.D. in New Testament Greek at the University of Aberdeen, Scotland, with the goal of teaching.)

From Tim, Our Fourth

I am the youngest member of this illustrious household. This means I am the major participant in many rituals which only those who also have held this position in their families will truly understand.

For example: "Hand-me-downs." This is a ritual best performed when an age span of at least five to ten years exists between siblings. In our family, brand-new, in-style clothes were originally bought for Steve (the modern-day blessing of the firstborn). He, of course, quickly outgrew these fanciful garments and new ones were dutifully purchased for him. The out-grown ones were then filed away for the next child, which in our case was Mike. Well, with both Mike and Mark around, more new clothes had to be bought, and they were, all to be filed away for that fateful day five years later when the last unsuspecting (and unexpected) member of the family entered the scene. To put it mildly, I inherited cases of ten-year-old clothes, all of which I had to wear out before I could experience the thrill of new clothes.

To further add to the trauma I was experiencing, these

clothes were all purchased in the '60s and early '70s . . . you do remember those styles, don't you? Polka dots, stripes, plaid, bell bottoms . . . to this day one of the most entertaining features of our family slides are the clothes we are wearing, and somehow almost all of them ended up in my wardrobe.

The second ritual of the lastborn I will refer to as "The Spoiled One." Here the entire family must participate. Everyone must let the youngest know that when they were growing up they never had it as good as I had it. We will start with my brothers' role. Mike and Mark made sure I knew, as they regularly wrestled me to the floor, that they never beat me up as bad as Steve beat them up. Mike would lie on me and tell me he was dead and I had to practice getting him off in case something like that really happened, while Mark would try out all his new wrestling moves on me, including once pinning me to the floor using no arms and no legs (he still brags about that).

Mike also stressed humility by beating me in three moves or less in chess, Stratego, or Risk. They also let me know that they never went to bed as late as I did, as I was tucked away at 7 P.M. with the rest of the family still up laughing and partying until all hours of the night . . . at least that was my perception. They also never had three or four pretzels in their lunch like me, as Mom packed them up with boxes of vanilla wafers, candy, and assorted snacks from Bates' nut farm for their two-hour trips to college. As for the parents' participation in "The Spoiled Child," they simply have to continue to bring up the subject of getting more than all the other siblings for the rest of the youngest's life. Just three to four weeks ago we somehow got on the same subject (I am now a college graduate).

The third ritual I will refer to as "The Picture Syndrome." The modern-day birthright (not blessing) of the firstborn is that parents seem to discover both the camera and how to bring babies into this world at the same time. Our family slides must consist of at least two full trays of Steve's baby pictures. They cover everything from haircuts to baths to playing with pots and pans; everything he did was so incredibly "cute" it had to be recorded with a photograph. By the time Mike came around things changed slightly and not everything needed to be remembered and some things had even lost their incredible cuteness. As Mark came along things got a little bit old; the combined total trays devoted to Mike's and Mark's infant days is probably one-and-a-half trays. Then I came along. Many things were no longer cute as they had once been. As a matter of fact, some of those incredibly "cute" things had become downright bothersome. Needless to say the photographic records of my childhood are not measured in trays. Simple numbers will suffice . . . very simple numbers.

As the youngest, it's easy to think of a lot of pressures that could have been placed on me or felt by me. It seems to me that it would have been normal for me to feel that I had to be as funny and quick-witted as Mark, as intelligent as Mike (straight *A*s through high school and college), or as successful as Steve (who was able to skip his last year of high school and go straight to college), but I never felt that I had to live up to their standards. Mom and Dad always accepted me for who I was, and as long as I was trying, my grades were not only acceptable but great in their sight, despite what my brothers had done.

I do remember many times wishing I was as smart as Mike or as funny as Mark, but those feelings were never a result of outside pressure put on me. It always seemed clear to me that I had my own special gifts and I never had to compete with my brothers.

Even when it came down to my choice of careers there was never any pressure. I remember wanting to be an engineer when I was growing up and my parents never discouraged that, which in turn made me want to use that desire in a way that they would be proud of, like using it on the mission field or in some other ministry/service.

I do remember one time being in Dad's study and at one point in the conversation he told me how he thought it would be really neat if I as the youngest also became a pastor. It may sound that it was said in a way that would make me feel pressure, but it wasn't. Dad said it in a way that made me feel extra special—I knew he was proud of me and saw good things in me that maybe were not as prevalent in my brothers.

It seemed to me often that Dad stuck up for me when I felt like the rest of the family was picking on me. I was always accepted by Dad, but it wasn't only a matter of acceptance—he was proud of me and he often expressed that.

I remember doing an object lesson in a Wednesday night service at our church as an example of what we did on a Mexico outreach trip. He made a special effort to be in to hear my part and I remember feeling that I had really not done a very good job. However, his comment at home was, "Looks like we have another speaker in the house." Times like that assured me that all I had to do was try hard and be myself and that would make my dad proud of me. Mom was also very encouraging and accepting but for some reason it meant more to me coming from Dad.

The time our family spent together was always so fun. The dinner table is a prime example of this. I couldn't count the number of times that by the end of dinner we would be laughing so hard that some of us would be literally rolling on the floor. I remember how fun it was when we played games together—Mom would usually fix root beer floats or some kind of milkshakes and we would all play Rook or Uno and at some point we would be dying laughing. This is a characteristic that still hasn't changed. Whenever we all get together it's like this.

I'm supposed to include in this whether I ever felt Mom and Dad were disappointed that I wasn't a girl. I think it's obvious by what I've already said that I never felt they were disappointed. Instead, I thought it was kind of funny that my name was going to be "Debbie Joy." Our family was always a source of security for me. I always knew Mom would be there when I got home from school, and I always felt comfortable with the family.

I enjoyed bringing friends over to our house, and Mom and Dad always accepted that. There were a lot of times while I was in high school when my friends and I would end up at our house to watch movies or play Risk. I remember whenever a James Bond movie was on TV on Sunday nights anywhere from six to twelve of my friends would come over after church to see it. It was basically assumed there would be a James Bond party at our house on such occasions and I can never remember Mom or Dad ever saying no. It was funny to see how some of my friends would be shocked at how normal and down-to-earth my parents were when they were over for the first time or two. Some of them couldn't imagine my dad in anything but a suit.

As for the rituals which are performed with the youngest: As I grew up, I saw that things weren't really as unfair as they seemed; as a matter of fact, I ended up being the tallest in our family. Because of growing so tall I had the joy of handing a lot of my old, unwanted clothes up to my older brothers. Revenge is sweet.

Neither Mike nor Mark ever challenge me in wrestling matches anymore, and when I try to start one they always have some excuse not to . . . I wonder why? Mike even refuses to play Stratego with me—I've only beaten him about fifteen times in a row. He recently gave in and played me again and I beat him twice.

Mom also faithfully packed me up with goodies as I went off to college just as she had done for my brothers. And when it came to pictures, Dad didn't have as many exciting things going on around the house as the kids moved out, so he often had to use up film . . . you can guess who was the lucky object of that left-over film. As we buzz through our family slides now and get to my teenage years, the comments are usually along the lines of, "Here we go again, Dad had to use up film!" Which he did. There are quite a few more pictures of my high school years than of Steve's.

The greatest gift that God has given me has been my family and parents who love Him more than anything else. I can't imagine where our family would be if my mom and dad had given up on their marriage – but because they stuck it out and worked it out I have seen and continue to see and experience a prime example of God's love for me.

I realize the security, joy and bond of unity that our family has is rare, but I also realize it's rare because so many couples give up when God has the strength available to produce the same characteristics in their home.

There is nobody in this world I would rather have for parents than my mom and dad. I love them and appreciate them more than I can say, and my prayer to God is that if I have a family some day, I, too, can model His love to my wife and kids as Mom and Dad did to me.

(Tim has graduated from Moody Bible Institute's missionary flight training program and is looking forward to a career in missionary aviation.)